DANGEROUS BOOKS FOR GIRLS

THE BAD REPUTATION OF ROMANCE NOVELS, EXPLAINED

MAYA RODALE

For the readers and writers of romance novels,
past, present and future

CONTENTS

FOREWORD

ARE ROMANCE NOVELS STILL DANGEROUS BOOKS?

I recently watched season two of Shonda Rhimes's adaptation of *Bridgerton* on Netflix, where for a moment, it was the most watched show ever. Dear Reader, I trust that I don't need to explain the significance of Shonda or Netflix or *Bridgerton* or what a heady combination of all those words in one sentence is for those of us who have been kicking around Romancelandia for some time, who have been in the trenches of blog comments, ferociously discussing whether lady readers have the brain power to distinguish between fantasy and reality. Now, we are recommending romances for Oprah and even *The New York Times* reviews romance novels. We've come a long way baby!

And just like that, I couldn't help but wonder: does romance still have a bad reputation?

Are romance novels still dangerous books for girls?

These days, there is a willingness for our culture at large to engage with the romance genre with a little less snark and a little more open-mindedness. Possibly unpopular hot take: I think we can thank *Fifty Shades of Grey*, which was too big for mainstream media to ignore, and the recently trendy illustrated covers, which make romance seem cute, chic, cool and thus "safe." We can also thank people at various media outlets who themselves are romance readers and who created space for the genre on their platforms.

I also think romance readers are more openly unapologetic in their love for the genre and have significantly less tolerance for other people's bullshit about our reading habits. Good. One simply cannot get away with slagging off the genre without attracting the ire of Romancelandia. It is not recommended to attract the ire of Romancelandia.

But I think the romance genre is still dangerous to patriarchal white supremacy, even as it can also be a tool to uphold it.

I first wrote *Dangerous Books For Girls: The Bad Reputation of Romance Novels, Explained* in 2010-ish, as my master's thesis and it was heavy on the origins of the novel and publishing industry as well as fears of delicate young white ladies getting ideas about their own autonomy (and anatomy). I rewrote it as a collection of essays and published that version in 2015, the heyday of *Fifty Shades of Grey*, Sheryl Sandberg's *Lean In* and the Obama years. How the world has changed since then.

This book was written before #MeToo and serious considerations around what it means to consent, before a serious reckoning about diversity, inclusion and representation in romance, before the spectacular implosion of Romance Writers of America (RWA). Before #WeNeedDiverseBooks and the tragic death of George Floyd and the reckoning it inspired. Before the pandemic and many other BFD and OMFG things that shall not be named.

In many ways, this book is dated. I intend to let it be so.

I cringe at how earnestly I celebrate *Lean In* without examining the racial and classist dimensions to the concept of women and work and their life choices. Or what it really even means to have a choice. In 2015, I was not familiar with Intersectional Feminism, which is "a prism for seeing the way in which various forms of inequality often operate together and exacerbate each other," according to Kimberlé Crenshaw, an American law professor who coined the term in 1989.

In 2015, I hadn't considered how "by women, about women, for women" is unnecessarily reductive and exclusionary. Not everyone strictly identifies as male or female, man or woman. Not every romance reader or writer identifies as a woman. The most recent stats I've seen show that 18% of the readership is male. Given the stigma surrounding men and romance, I have a hunch that number is much higher. Good! And while the romance novel has historically been portrayed as the domain of white, heterosexual women, we ought to ask if it should be or needs to be (probably not). What does a romance genre look like when there is space for all kinds of identities?

From 2017 to 2021, I had the honor and privilege of reviewing romance novels for NPR. Every month, I sifted through dozens and dozens of pitches for new releases. I discovered new authors and books on Twitter. And I made it a point to read beyond my usual go-to's of Regency historical romance. I also made it a point to read more diverse books by diverse authors and featuring characters of color, those who identify as LGBTQIA+ or those who are differently-abled. For every three books I reviewed in my monthly column, there were a dozen that I started but didn't quite make the cut, but overall I read a lot of great romance novels. It was a joy to recommend them to other readers.

By reading so widely, I have come to understand that the romance genre isn't just empowering to women; it is empowering to any marginalized group in the same way. It does so by giving them authority over their stories, visibility on their terms, nuanced and empathetic depictions of characters, unapologetic joy on the page and the happy ever after. The genre provides a framework to tell stories that empower.

We are collectively redefining what "happy ever after" (HEA) looks like. It is no longer just marriage and babies. And when the HEA is no longer about just marriage and just babies, we can write romance novels about people for whom marriage and babies do not necessarily apply. Queer historicals, for example. Or women beyond childbearing years. In Romancelandia, we have adopted the "happy for now" (HFN) ending, which may not have wedding rings and sleeping babies, but definitely has an emotionally uplifting and optimistic conclusion, which is what really matters. To me, the HFN means more happiness for more characters.

But as I write this new forward, *Roe v. Wade* has recently been overturned, stripping away a constitutional right to bodily autonomy from half the population. There are also horrendous efforts to curtail LGBTQIA+ and Trans rights. Books are being banned from school libraries—often books that celebrate love and diversity. Too many people in America still wake up wondering if they are considered fully human in the eyes of the law and society. The world is such that many of us need a break from the doomscrolling; we need to get lost in the pages of a romance novel.

Many defenses of the romance genre begin with the fact that it's a billion dollar industry. I have written more than a few of those myself, but no longer. Romance is valuable because—full stop. No genre—or human—needs to justify it's worth by the amount of money it makes. But it's still important to consider the connection between romance novels and money and value.

When a person writes a romance novel, when a publisher buys a romance novel, when a reader gives their time to a romance novel, a statement is being made about who is considered lovable and who is considered valuable. I do mean actual cash value—a writer's time, a publisher's advance, a reader's money.

Historically, the genre has been a safe space for women to define and create their own value. We have written novels about women, which have sold well, which have put money in the pockets of lady authors, which has given them power and allowed them to expand the market. Rinse, repeat.

It is important that other presently marginalized groups get to define and create their own value via romance. It is important that these books get the attention of reviewers and shelf space and that these authors get money in their pockets. It is important that readers and authors help expand this market. Rinse, repeat.

Authors and readers: we are not passive participants in this. We make choices when we write and when, and what, we read. We send a message when we purchase a book, review it and tell our friends. When a person writes a romance novel, we are making a statement about who we believe is lovable. Are HEAs really only for dukes and other rich white men (unless you're in Shondaland)? What are we saying when we write novels romancing cops and billionaires? Does love really only exist in the eleven years of Regency England and fictional small towns in contemporary America? Who deserves a happy ever after?

On a similar note, we are also making statements about truth, love and value in historical fiction and romance when we make claims about "historical accuracy." This edition includes a new essay, *The Truth About Historical Accuracy: The Subversive Work of Historical Fiction*, which examines this idea especially as it pertains to the history of women and other marginalized groups and how they are represented—or not—in our genre.

When Shonda made her version of *Bridgerton*, it gave us all a lot to talk about, especially her colorblind casting. There was an explosion of think pieces about Black people in the Regency and the truth about Queen Charlotte. We did research and we all learned something—the Regency wasn't as white as we might have thought. The duke was Black and the romance still worked. We had earnest conversations in the comments of social media posts about whether it mattered that the book said the duke had blue eyes and then Regé-Jean Page made us realize it did not matter. We had a debate about what Daphne does to Simon and the stunning lack of consent. We compared the original printed pages to the TV show.

And just like that, we all know a little more about race and the Regency, about consent, and space has been made in the minds of readers for more stories that incorporate this new knowledge. The formula and the framework held, and the genre and the readership moved forward.

So, are romance novels still dangerous? Only if you are trying to hold on to a past that never really existed.

I believe that the romance novel format is as subversive as ever, even as it is no longer a shy, Regency lady worried about her reputation. The romance genre these days feels like a heroine who is still not quite Respectable, but it doesn't matter because she has a circle of those who love her, for herself, just the way she is. Clinch, flaws, scandal and all. Now she moves through the world with the confidence and freedom that comes from being openly, nakedly, unapologetically loved. May she use her power to create a happy ever after for all.

PREFACE

When my mother first insisted that I read romance novels, I laughed. She couldn't seriously be suggesting that I, a college student at a prestigious East Coast university majoring in English, who read *Ulysses* for school and all of Proust for fun, would read one of those cheap drugstore books, the Fabio books, the fluffy reading material for uneducated and overweight desperate housewives of the flyover states.

But she was serious. She pointed out that as a student focusing on women's roles in fiction, both as writers and characters, I couldn't possibly refuse to study the most popular and profitable books by women, for women, about women.

"Fine," I grumbled, wanting to be a diligent academic. "Send me a syllabus."

She did. I started with Jane Austen, reading her collected works in a nearby park. I moved onto *Forever Amber* by Kathleen Windsor and was furious with the ending. I couldn't get into *Shanna* by Kathleen Woodiwiss, but I was so absorbed by *The Flame and the Flower* that I took a taxi rather than walk to meet a friend just so I could keep reading. From there, I tried out newer romances by Susan Elizabeth Phillips, Eloisa James, and others. In my entire academic career, I had never moved through a syllabus so quickly and happily.

Deep down, this was exactly what I had been afraid of. I suspected that I would enjoy romance novels so much that I would be ruined for "real books." I envisioned myself dropping out of school with no prospects, romantic or professional, with nothing but a giant stack of mass-market paperback romance novels to fill my days and nights. A terrible fate indeed.

Nevertheless, I got hooked on reading romance novels and still managed to graduate from college, write a book with my mom, go to graduate school, and get a job. Along the way, I started writing and publishing my own historical romance novels (dedication in the first one: *Momma, this is all your fault*). I joined the trade organization Romance Writers of America. I made smart new friends and met my favorite authors.

But through the years, a question nagged at me: When my mom insisted that I read romances, how did I know to laugh when I had never read one?

We didn't have romances lying around the house—in fact, my mom had only just started reading them. I didn't know anyone else who read them—or so I thought. I hadn't read reviews or noticed advertisements for them. I hadn't really seen them in the supermarkets or bookstores. I hadn't even flipped through one to giggle at the sexy bits.

But somehow I just *knew* that smart girls didn't read the Fabio books, and I had a whole bunch of other unflattering assumptions about the books and readership.

How I inherently knew these things—and in fact, I've pondered whether they are true—is a question I've been trying to answer for the past 10 years. It has inevitably lead to more questions about whether I, as a romance novelist, was writing empowering stories or ones that tricked women into traditional, limiting gender roles. Was there any value in my life's work or was I devoting my time and energy to something frivolous when I could be earning more money at a Real Job? Why did I read and write about first kisses and happily-ever-afters over and over again?

This book is my answer.

In college, my professors allowed me to add a few romance novels to the list of great books for my final project. In graduate school, I studied women's fiction from early eighteenth and nineteenth century England. In fact, my master's thesis was an early version of this book. I wrote extensively (ten historical romances, three contemporary romances, and countless blogs). I read widely, including a lot of romance.

In addition to a decade's worth of reading, studying, writing, and thinking, I drew extensively on one-on-one interviews and the results of two surveys I conducted for this book.

About the surveys: The first questionnaire for romance readers was a whopper and asked everything from basic demographic information (age, marital status, level of education, etc.) to readers' thoughts on character traits they prefer, why they love reformed rakes, what is their preferred heat levels in romances, and whether they feel ashamed to be seen reading "trashy books" in public. The survey was shared widely on social media by myself and others in the romance community. As of this writing, more than 800 people have taken it. It was not meant to be a truly scientific study but a way to solicit the thoughts and feelings of a large number of romance readers.

I also conducted a smaller survey of non-romance readers, asking such questions as "how would you describe a romance novel" or "how would you describe romance readers" because I wanted to see if the stereotypes about the books and readers were widely held, or if romance readers were over-sensitive and perceiving slights where there were none.

From both surveys I learned that there is undeniably a negative perception of the genre, and its readers and romance fans were all aware of it.

Links to the surveys and downloadable versions of the results are available at www.dangerousbooksforgirls.com.

Here's one of the things I love about the romance commu-nity: The members are so smart, funny, opinionated, *and* willing to share. Through a series of interviews conducted in coffee shops and over the phone, I spoke with bestselling authors, senior editors, editorial assistants, scholars, cover artists, and journalists. Each person took an hour (or more) out of their busy days to have a conversation with me about the romance genre. Unless attributed to another source, quotes in this book were taken from these interviews.

This book is organized by themes. The chapters are presented in loose chronological order, but readers should feel free to read them in any order that strikes their fancy.

When I sign books, I often scribble "happy reading" to readers or in notes to authors I add "happy writing!" When

we get past the sense of shame or snark that is often directed
at the genre, that is what romance is about for so many of us:
a sense of happiness, joy, acceptance, and love. It is about the
ability of a good story to both entertain and empower us.

ONE

WHAT WE TALK ABOUT WHEN WE TALK ABOUT FABIO

WHEN I MENTION that I write romance novels at cocktail parties, one of the most frequent responses from men and women alike is "Oh, like the Fabio books?"

When the *New Yorker* wrote about HarperCollins's recent acquisition of Harlequin[1] to the tune of $450 million, a significant portion of the post wasn't about the deal or the genre, but…Fabio!

When the popular reality show *America's Next Top Model* wanted to take on the modeling challenge of a romance novel cover photo shoot, they enlisted…Fabio! After all, in the words of Tyra Banks, he is "Mr. Romance Novel himself."

When I asked non-romance readers to describe a romance novel in their own words, more than a few wrote "Fabio!"—exclamation mark and all.

Fabio, of course, is the hunky model who has appeared on more than 400 romance novel covers, including classics like Johanna Lindsay's *Gentle Rogue* and *Savage Thunder*. He defines the stereotypical cover model for which the genre is infamous—a hulking, muscle-bound man with his billowing white shirt open to the waist but still tucked into buff-colored breeches. His hair is long and blonde and flowing in a fake breeze. A busty young woman clings to him as her breasts spill out of her bodice.

After those covers, he launched a hugely successful career as a model and spokesperson, even publishing his own romances. He's so well known that people who know *nothing* about romance novels know to say "Fabio!" when the subject comes up.

"It's an amazing bit of branding that people are still so quick to make that association," says Esi Sogah, a senior romance editor at Kensington and a person who also gets the "Fabio!" response when mentioning romance novels at cocktail parties.

Romance novels are a billion dollar industry—and they're the largest segment of adult fiction, outselling fantasy, mystery, science fiction, and the classics.[2] Thousands of titles are published each year for millions of readers. All of them are predominantly written by women, for women, and about women. They are largely produced by women, too; the publishing workforce is 74 percent female, according to a survey by *Publisher's Weekly*.[3]

And yet the romance novel is so often reduced to and personified by one man.

Fabio.

Honestly, I offer my sincere congrats to Fabio. From interviews and profiles I've read, he seems like a very nice, sincere guy. And what success! Even decades after his last cover, people at cocktail parties are still asking me if Fabio, now 56, has modeled for my recent books.

I am happy for him and his success. I even like his work.

But why is such a massively powerful and profitable female-driven industry exemplified by a dude?

THERE IS and has been much angst about romance novels long before Fabio unbuttoned his shirt and stepped in front of the fan. More than just stories of girl meets boy, these novels embody and explore topics our culture is deeply uncomfortable with.

Romances tackle divisive issues like class, love, women's sexuality and pleasure, rape, virginity, money, feminism, masculinity, and equality—and ultimately how they're all tangled up with each other. These books promote a woman's right to make choices about her own life (and body). They take longstanding notions of masculinity and turn them around. They promote a different image of what it means to be a happy, desirable woman—one that doesn't rely on the right shade of lipstick, but internal qualities instead. These books celebrate women who get out of the house and do all the things that, traditionally, young ladies and good girls don't do.

Rather than suggesting a woman needs a man or that the sexes are at war, romance novels demonstrate again and again that true happiness happens when two people find and prioritize love.

Most scandalous of all, these are books by women, for women, and about women in a culture that doesn't place much value on women.

So when the subject of romance novels—and all those knotty issues—comes up, we talk about Fabio instead of women's orgasms or men's feelings.

We laugh about Fabio's very fitted breeches instead of asking who is watching the children or cooking dinner while a woman reads privately for pleasure or writes a romance novel or is out at work. Simply by picking one up, she is refusing, if only for a chapter, her traditional role of caring for others, and in doing so she declares that *she* is important.

It's easier to talk about Fabio's pectoral muscles than to talk about how successful women can be when they're working and working together.

It's easier to laugh about the bodice Fabio is ripping than to have an honest discussion about women's sexual pleasure or to even acknowledge women's sexual desires. After all, sex isn't polite cocktail party conversation.

Rather than discuss all that, we can just talk about one, supremely masculine man and the way the wind blows through his long, flowing hair.

Maybe it's what we *don't* talk about when we talk about Fabio.

ROMANCE NOVELS ARE MORE than just Fabio books. They are also more than bodice rippers, mommy porn, trashy books, rescue fantasies, guilty pleasures, or any of the other "funny" but disparaging slang terms we have for them. For centuries, they have been the work of "that damned mob of scribbling women," to quote that infamous line from Nathaniel Hawthorne, and they have been a source of private pleasure for millions more. For a majority of readers, they are escape, entertainment, and happiness. Romance novels have been—and still are—the dangerous books that show women again and again that they're worth it.

And you thought it was just about Fabio.

THE REPUTATION OF ROMANCE NOVELS

Shhh...

51%

of readers have felt they
should keep their romance
reading secret

85% AND **89%**

of readers think   think romance
romance has a   readers are
bad reputation   looked down on

191   2

Number of   Number of
New York Times   New York Times
Bestsellers   Book Reviews
Nora Roberts   of Nora's books
has written

67%

think romance novels don't
get the respect they deserve

WHY?

Because women
read it and write it

Because sex

Because feelings

Just 1% think romance novels get
the respect they deserve.

62%   **50%**

think romance   of romance
novels are   readers love the
empowering to   genre and don't
women   care who knows it

**Less than 1% think they are
degrading to women**

Sources: The New York Times, The Dangerous Books For Girls study.

TWO

THE ROMANCE REVOLUTION

THE REAL REASONS ROMANCE NOVELS GET EVERYONE'S UNMENTIONABLES IN A TWIST

And no matter what anybody says, I don't believe all this trouble started when women got the vote. As far as I'm concerned, it goddamn well started when you taught each other how to read.
   —*Fancy Pants* by Susan Elizabeth Phillips

WHETHER WE CALL THEM GOTHICS, domestic fiction, sentimental novels, chick-lit, trashy books, romances, or romance novels,[1] affordable novels written by women, about women, and for women have promoted powerful and revolutionary messages to women for centuries.

Today the commonly accepted definition of a romance novel is the one created by trade organization Romance Writers of America: a novel with a central love story and an emotionally satisfying and optimistic conclusion.[2] These are stories in which two individuals come to a greater understanding of themselves through a romantic relationship. It is virtually guaranteed that no children, dogs, heroes, or heroines will die. There are obstacles and dark moments when all seems lost before ending happily.

To understand the power of these books, we have to consider not just the themes championed over and over again, but the context in which these stories arose and proliferated. The eighteenth and nineteenth centuries were rife with revolutions—the American, the French, the Industrial—and it was understood that they were fueled by widespread reading.

Who was reading and what they were reading was particularly concerning. "Reading—and the novel in particular—was very much associated with the promotion of ideas which might lead to fundamental changes in the status quo, including the position of women," writes Belinda Jack in her book *The Woman Reader*.[3] Stories of personal transformation and social change presented a powerful image of how the social norm could be altered for greater happiness.

But some certain reading material (ahem, novels) were considered more seditious than others. It was generally accepted in the eighteenth and nineteenth centuries that novels were supposed to be as true to life as possible. But because they were still fictional works, there were fears that they could be mistaken for reality or assumed to be possible in a way that more obviously fantastical stories could not.

Novels were also considered to be trouble because women were fond of reading them. One strategy to blunt the effects of novels on women was to make sure that women were at least reading the *right* thing, such as texts that reinforced traditional ideas of femininity and women's roles. "Once women were reading in significant numbers—and this is true across cultures—reading material telling them how to behave appeared more or less simultaneously," writes Jack. Conduct books and collections of sermons became perennial bestsellers. They not only gave advice on how one ought to

behave (like a good little girl), but they also started to establish the connection that one learns how to live a good life
from books—something we may take for granted now.

When novels came along, there were real fears that
women would take their cues from these "ridiculous" books
instead of more respectable books. "We incline to think that a
far larger number of persons receive the bias of their course
and the complexion of their character from reading novels
than from hearing sermons," one nineteenth century author
wrote.[4] Not only that, but there were genuine concerns that
women would develop unrealistic expectations about their
lives by reading fiction. Another nineteenth century author
painted a dire picture: "She [the novel reader] dreamed and
spoke of splendid matches, 'til she became quite unfitted of
the matter-of-fact world in which her lot was cast."[5]

In order to stop the spread of these revolutionary ideas
through books to disenfranchised people, the government in
England enacted legislation called "the taxes on knowledge."
First, the Stamp Act of 1712 made printed materials expensive, hoping to price them out of the hands of women and
poor people. Taxes were placed on paper and advertisements,
so "the bigger the book, the bigger the tax."[6] Similarly, the
stamp duties on newspapers and pamphlets were understood
to be "targeted attacks on the reading matter which the state
feared most."[7]

The window tax—which one had to pay on any more than
six windows in one dwelling—made free reading light (sun-
light) expensive. Long hours at the factory meant people were
too exhausted to read even if they saved up for a book and a
candle. Charles Dickens claimed that this was the most effective of all the taxes on knowledge.[8]

When those measures failed—they weren't repealed until
1855—snark and scorn were deployed to diminish literature

that appealed to women. Critics elevated intellectual literature composed by educated white males and denigrated anything that was mass produced or created by females.

As a result, "those books" became impolite conversation. By being made to feel ashamed of their reading materials, women didn't read them or if they did, they didn't talk about it—thus potentially smothering the primary way other women could discover them. If they weren't reviewed in the paper— and they weren't—you might find them though a friend's recommendation, unless your friend wasn't admitting to the collection of embarrassing romances stashed in her bedside table drawer.

But neither the taxes on knowledge or mockery on a massive scale was enough to stop this scourge of novel reading. The revolution carried on as women continued to read and write the novels that appealed to them, despite being subjected to snark—if they were regarded at all.

In 1858, Wilkie Collins lamented the discovery of the "unknown reading public" that read for amusement rather than information (horrors). Mocking the medium as formulaic and unrealistic and its audience for being stupid was a way to minimize the impact of the ideas within. So much so that even today women who read and love romances will call them "trashy books" or "smutty books." That is, if they talk about it at all.

Fortunately, women did talk. And read. And write. By creating stories with an intense focus on a heroine—her choices, her pleasure, her independence, *and her rewards*— romance novels promoted radical ideas of what a woman could do with her life and inspired women to try to make that dream a reality. Far more than "silly novels by silly novelists," these books are perhaps some of the most subversive literature ever written, distributed, and consumed.

And you thought it was all about Prince Charming.

Six reasons romance novels are dangerous books

#1 Because women

"There were knights!" she cried. "I can still be a knight!"
"No, you can't," he said, more patient than ever because she was so sadly confused. "You're a girl. Girls can't be knights."
She snatched the sketchbook from his hands and swung it at his head.
—*Lord Perfect* by Loretta Chase

So many of the Great Stories in the literary canon, or on movie screens, or in books are about boys, from Virgil and Odysseus to King Arthur, Ulysses, and Spiderman. The girl, when she appeared in stories, was often there because of her relationship to the men: She was the wife, the mother, the girlfriend, the sassy best friend. She was and is the Other. Even today, women have only 31 percent of speaking roles in movies, and many of these are what one writer at Slate deemed "reactress" roles in which female stars play parts that "require little more than glumly registering the drama dished out by their male counterparts." [9]

"The romance novel puts the heroine at the center of the book, at least coequal to the hero, or occupying more of the spotlight than he does. Her desires are central," writes professor Pamela Regis in her book *A Natural History of the Romance Novel*, one of the early, seminal works of scholarship on the genre. In a romance novel, the heroine is Odysseus, Aeneas, etc. She is the reader's avatar and her guide on a journey. This in itself is audacious, because it asserts that women are worthy of a reader's interest, attention, and trust for hundreds of pages, that she is equal to a man (at least in the pages of a book), that she is capable of a transformative journey, that she is more than an empty vessel. She is enough.

For a woman to star in a novel, with all the conflict, drama, adventure, and romance that implies, suggested that there was more to a woman's existence than sitting at home minding the babies, the stove, and the sewing. Long before *Sex and the City*, single women were a source of angst because they don't quite *belong* to anyone. Most romance novels focus on the time period *before* marriage, when she has left the nursery but hasn't yet gotten married. She's not a girl, but not yet a woman.

Romance fiction "tells the story that reflects a woman's reality as it could be and as it is," Jennifer Crusie, a bestselling contemporary romance author, writes on her blog. "It tells her she is not stupid because she's female, that she understands men better than they understand her, that she has a right to control over her own life, to children, to vocational fulfillment, to great sex, to a faithful loving partner."[10] Romantic fiction relentlessly declares that women are worthy and their interests are valid and it is worth it for them to pursue their own happiness.

Elyse Discher, a romance reviewer with the romance blog Smart Bitches, Trashy Books, says romance resonated with her because "I had not been reading a lot of fiction up to that point that was representative of a young woman's feeling of being valid."

Too often, women do not prioritize their own happiness because they are so busy caring for others and trying to have it all. "Well, just reading one is an act in and of itself that

demonstrates that you care about yourself," writes Sarah
Wendell, blogger of Smart Bitches, Trashy Books in her book
*Everything I Know about Love I Learned from Romance
Novels*. "If you're like me, there's hardly a moment in your
day when you're not doing six things simultaneously. If
you're reading, then you're likely doing that one, indulgent
thing." Readers cite entertainment, escape, and relaxation as
the top reasons they read romance novels.

But it goes deeper than that. In the eighteenth and nineteenth centuries, reading was often done as a group—
someone might read to the whole family after supper, for
example. For that reason, the literature that did best commercially was the literature that was suitable for and interesting
to women. "At a time when many books bought individually
were collectively read within the family, any books which the
reviews declared unsuitable for ladies were commercially
sunk,"[11] writes William St Clair in his book *The Reading
Nation in the Romantic Period*. In this scenario, a man in the
family could still interrupt the reading and pronounce judgments on the characters, their actions, and the story.

However, as ideas of privacy started to take hold—as
physical *space* for privacy became more common—women
began reading alone. The text went straight to her brain and
her heart; it was not mediated or interpreted by a man or
anyone else. It was just a woman, writing for a woman, about
a woman who triumphs over the obstacles holding her back
from true happiness.

This can be a wonderful respite for a woman—but scary
if you were counting on her to pick you up after school or
greet you at the door with a martini.

#2 Because the love match

If one didn't have love, was it better, then, to be alone?
—*To Sir Phillip, with Love* by Julia Quinn

The hallmark of the romance novel is the love-match marriage. Today we take for granted the idea of marrying for love, but once upon a time, marriage was just about "the merging and protection of assets," to quote Miranda Hobbs, Esquire, of *Sex and the City.* Marriage was something you did for land, wealth, status, or more camels. The idea of actually liking the person you were going to spend the rest of your life with wasn't really an important consideration.

Being a person in possession of a vagina meant that *you* and your hopes, dreams, and wishes weren't often a consideration either. And why would they be? For most of human history, a woman couldn't own property, get a divorce, or even have custody over children she conceived, carried and delivered. In the eyes of the law, she wasn't even a person. Thus, how could a woman have thoughts and desires of her own? If she did, why would anyone care?

But then the idea of the love-match or companionate marriage began to take off. We can thank the Industrial Revolution and Big Government for this one. In her book, *Marriage, a History: How Love Conquered Marriage,* Stephanie Coontz writes,

For centuries, marriage did much of the work that markets and governments do today. It organized the production and distribution of goods and people. It set up political, economic, and military alliances. It coordinated the division of labor by gender and age. It orchestrated people's personal rights and obligations in everything from sexual relations to the inheritance of property. Most societies had very specific rules about how people should arrange their marriages to accomplish these tasks.[12]

Building on this in his book *The Science of Happily Ever After: What Really Matters in the Quest for Enduring Love*, author Ty Tashiro attributes the shift to "significant changes in life expectancy, reproductive health, and wealth." As more people simply got enough calories in a day and had more children survive to adulthood, marriage could be about something other than finding someone (literally) with the strength and resources to get through the day, plus enough left over to reproduce and nurture children into adulthood.

As more people had more energy (thanks to getting enough to eat), more money (thanks to increased productivity), and more security (thanks to the government), people simply had more time and energy to focus on other pursuits— like love. Marriage had a chance to be about something else. This is not to say that people hadn't fallen in love before or experienced deep emotions, but there was now a shift in priorities when one was considering a spouse.

That romance novels are often understood to be about "getting married and living happily ever after" gets them a bad rap from some feminists. Pamela Regis summarizes this critique: "The marriage, they claim, enslaves the heroine and, by extension, the reader...Its ending destroys the independent, questing woman depicted in the rest of the story."[13]

But what is really happening, in real life and in novels, is that women were finally getting to make choices about their personal lives. Elevating love meant elevating personal considerations above considerations like wealth or status. It also meant elevating the personal lives of women. "Her choice to marry the hero is just one manifestation of her freedom," Regis writes. And, I should point out, it is nearly always the heroine's choice (except in books that employ an arranged marriage or marriage of convenience tropes).

But just as women were being told that it was okay to marry for love, they also had more practical things to consider, like economic security. The titular heroine of *Belinda,* an 1801 novel, strikes this balance between the emotional and practical considerations of marriage: "I am not so romantic as to imagine that I could be happy with you, or you with me, if we were in absolute want of the common comforts of life."[14]

Of course, it would be convenient if one could fall in love with a wealthy man, but this wasn't always a case. While speaking about the science and history of love on a panel at a conference on romance at the Library of Congress, scholar Stephanie Coontz told the audience, "As a result of these tensions [between love and economic security], women came to experience romance as a tangled bundle of mystery and unpredictability." A romance novel was the perfect, low-risk way to explore and negotiate these tensions.

In reality, marriage for love did not necessarily lead to happily ever after. "The insistence that marriage be based on true love and companionship spurred some to call for further liberalization of divorce laws," Coontz writes in her book on marriage. "To them, a loveless union was immoral and ought to be dissolved without dishonor. The strongest opponents of divorce in the nineteenth century were traditionalists who disliked the exaltation of married love. They feared that making married love the center of people's emotional lives would raise divorce rates, and they turned out to be right."[15]

The problems with the love-match didn't stop there. If a couple was able to divorce, how would a woman be able to support herself? She would need financial independence and thus she would have to abandon her station as angel of the house and go out to work, possibly taking jobs from men. Who, then, is minding the children?

If love is the primary reason to marry, and love doesn't care about class distinctions, skin color, or even gender, it inevitably raises questions of who should be allowed to marry whom. Many historically set romances derive their conflicts from lovers in separate social classes.

The widespread acceptance and recognition of love as a reason to marry took a while. Interracial marriage wasn't legalized in the United States until 1967. We've only just begun to legalize gay marriage in the United States and as of this writing, there are still states that arguing against it.

Over time, love has forced a reevaluation of traditional concepts of marriage. It has led to the transition from an older system of "arranged, patriarchal marriage" to "the love-based male breadwinner marriage, with its ideal of lifelong monogamy and intimacy," as Coontz writes. And even that is still in flux. But recognizing love has been the first step toward acknowledging the rights and humanity of more than just powerful, heterosexual, white men.

#3 Because escape

> *If adventures do not befall a lady in her own village, she must seek them abroad.*
> —*Northanger Abbey* by Jane Austen

Romance novels then and now are all about women getting out of the house. From ballrooms to boardrooms, they declare that a woman's place is not just in the home. One of the classic early romance novels, *Evelina* by Fanny Burney, bears the subtitle: *A young woman's entrance into the world.* On the flip side, gothic romances are horror stories about a young woman trapped inside a house.

Getting out of the house symbolizes stepping away from a dull, predictable life of low expectations and choosing to go on a risky journey that might lead to unimaginable happiness or utter ruination.

It is when Cinderella goes to the ball. It is when Cornelia Litchfield Case ditches the White House in Susan Elizabeth Phillip's *First Lady*. It is when Miss Olivia Wingate-Carsington and Peregrine Dalmay, Earl of Lisle, embark on outrageously grand road trips in Loretta Chase's novels *Lord Perfect* and *Last Night's Scandal*. It is the heroine who agrees to the sham marriage, just one kiss, just one night of pleasure, just one adventure.

Mobility became a key feature in the early novels, whether in *The History of Tom Jones, a Foundling* (1749) by Henry Fielding or the physical and symbolic journey undertaken by the titular heroine of the novel *Clarissa* by Samuel Richardson, in which she goes from being locked in her parents' house to being locked in a house of ill repute. We see it in *Pride and Prejudice* when Elizabeth goes to traveling with her aunt and uncle. As her physical location changes and she sees more of the world and the man, her feelings for Darcy are transformed.

At a time when most people never traveled farther than the local village and women weren't allowed to travel alone, this mobility was momentous. In later romance novels, heroines are kidnapped and dragged all over the American West (*Sweet Savage Love*), or they gallivant between continents (in *Shanna*, the heroine is in England, the Caribbean, and America). In paranormal romances, characters exist in or travel between fantastical worlds. Mobility was employed as a "teachable moment" for geography, other cultures, or character development.

This became a point of concern for critics of the novel. Since novels were supposed to be realistic portrayals of life, readers were in grave danger of being misled by a lady novelist who wrote about faraway lands she'd never traveled to and about people, the likes of whom she'd never meet—all from the safety of her drawing room. A female's sheltered existence was why these novels written by ladies were discredited. But they were an appealing escape for young ladies stuck in the drawing room.

Even more troubling to critics was the portrayal of social mobility portrayed in romances. The Industrial Revolution and the rising middle class blurred the lines between High and Low/Us and Them. With an increasing number of people with money and the elevation of love as a criterion for marriage, the idea of marrying outside of one's social class became increasingly acceptable.

The classic example is Samuel Richardson's epic best-seller, *Pamela: Or, Virtue Rewarded* (1740), in which a virtuous housemaid eventually married the lord of the manor. Even though they are married and in love, the novel continues for another hundred pages in which we see Pamela struggling to win over the local high society. The idea of a housemaid rising to the status of lady of the manor was so shocking, nearly a quarter of the book was needed to explain it. Many, many romances, then and now, feature impoverished women landing a wealthy spouse, from *Pride & Prejudice* to *Fifty Shades of Grey*.

This is an example of why the critics were upset with these novels and the women who read them. They gave a girl ideas about what she might expect from her life that were contrary to what everyone else was telling her. In a mid-nineteenth century essay "What Girls Read," Edward G. Salmon writes about the dangers of women reading these cheap stories:

We do not often see an account of a girl committing any very serious fault through her reading. But let us go into the houses of the poor, and try to discover what is the effect on the maiden mind of the trash which maidens buy. If we were to trace the matter to its source, we should probably find that the high-flown conceits and pretentions of the poor girls of the period, their dislike of manual work and love of freedom, spring largely from notions imbibed in the course of a perusal of their penny fictions. Their conduct towards their friends, their parents, their husbands, their employers, is colored by what they then gather. They obtain distorted views of life, and the bad influence of these works on themselves is handed down to their children and scattered broadcast throughout the family.[16]

With these pleasant and affordable—but highly sugges-tive—novels, women were able to read about the world beyond their immediate experiences. They could see more than the view from the drawing room window and encounter more types of people than the folks in the village.

These different types of mobility portrayed in novels send the same message to the reader: Your here and now is not your forever. Your situation on page one is not where you'll end up in the epilogue. The narrative arc, in which a character grows and transforms, drives home this idea that your birth is not your destiny.

These books broadened the reader's understanding of what the world was and could be, and then suggested, with every grand adventure and happy ending, that their lives could be so much richer and more fulfilling...if they only just venture out of the house.

#4 Because women become the author-ity

> *Upon the demise of her first marriage, Julianna turned to writing. She wrote for money. She wrote for her dignity. She wrote to keep a roof over her head, to feed her belly and fire up her soul. She wrote to pay for her late husband's indiscretions. She wrote so that she would be beholden to no one.*
>
> —*A Tale of Two Lovers* by Maya Rodale

"Women...are the chief readers of novels; they are also, of late at least, the chief writers of them. A great proportion of these authoresses too are young ladies," William Rathbone Greg writes in 1859 in an article for the *National Review* on the "false morality of lady novelists."

That women read and write these novels has lead to the notion of romances being "women's work" and it has been devalued accordingly, in the same way as teachers, nurses, and other "typically female" dominated industries. But there are a few additional reasons why lady novelists are of particular concern to the critics.

First, some of the disdain was reserved for the form of the novel itself. "Oh, it's only a novel," Jane Austen writes, undoubtedly with sarcasm, in *Northanger Abbey*. It is only "some work in which the greatest powers of the mind are displayed, in which the most thorough knowledge of human nature, the happiest delineation of its varieties, the liveliest effusions of wit and humour, are conveyed to the world in the best-chosen language."

Second, women in the eighteenth and nineteenth centuries had limited education and experience in comparison to men. If novels were to be realistic and accurate representations of real life, then how could these Lady Authors, whose "experi-ence in life is seldom wide and never deep" do this well? How could honorable and virtuous young women write cred-ibly about passions? (And God forbid she wrote it from first-hand experience.) Even if women did manage to write well-plotted stories with "pleasing sentiments" and well-drawn characters, the Lady Author was still doomed to fail simply because of her sex: "The views of life and the judgments of conduct must be imperfect and superficial, and will often be thoroughly unsound."[17]

It was also thought that if women must be doing this in their spare time with little education or formal training, then it must be hackwork. "There are vast numbers of lady novelists, for much the same reason that there are vast numbers of semptresses [seamstresses]," Greg writes. "Thousands of women have nothing to do and yet are under the necessity of doing something." This perception was hardly helped by the sheer volume of such novels published then and now.

But all this criticism hardly stopped women from reading and writing such novels. Greg writes "the supply of the fiction market has mainly fallen into their hands" and today romance accounts for most fiction sold in the United States. What does this mean? Money.

Many women throughout history have found writing a suitable way to work from home. As much as romance novels were stories of women embarking on adventures out of the house, it was a job one could do while running a household, especially since mass production of household goods during the Industrial Revolution freed up some of women's time. (We see this again later in the 1950s and 1960s when new labor-saving appliances freed up so much of a housewife's time that it spurred many to join the workforce.)

Writing then gave women a semi-respectable way of

earning money while still largely upholding a traditional role. "We had imagined that destitute women turned novelists, as they turned governesses, because they had no other 'lady-like' means of getting their bread," George Eliot writes in her essay *Silly Novels by Lady Novelists*. Two of the bestselling American lady novelists that everyone seems to have forgotten, E.D.E.N. Southworth, author of *The Hidden Hand, or Capitola the Madcap,* and Susan Warner, author of the massive bestseller *The Wide, Wide World*, supported their families with their popular and prolific writing about tragic girls left to make their way alone in the world, twists of fate, and reversals of fortune. And those are just two examples.

Women wrote themselves into positions of authority. On one hand, this demand for books for women, about women, and by women helped launch a whole new marketplace in which women were—and are—principal players. This meant money, which translated to more power in the household, or even the ability to leave it.

But this position of authority manifested in other ways. When women wrote stories about women and their experiences, it was a topic of which they were experts, or at least more expert than men. And when women wrote, they often created stories where men are brought around to love, respect, understand, and value a woman. Rather than wait for outside validation by a man, each story written by a woman, about a woman, who declared their worth.

A writer is God and Queen, Lord and Master of her fictional world. She controls the weather, every heartbeat, every breath, every thought, and the fates of fictional people.

It's no small thing for a woman to have the experience of writing a story where she has power over an entire (fictional) world, especially when she may not have it in her real life.

#5 Because female orgasms

> *Hell, at this rate she'd end up in the mental institution by*
> *the end of the year. Cause: Celibacy.*
> —*The Marriage Bargain* by Jennifer Probst

The novel, and by extension the lady novel by a lady novelist, was born in the age of revolutions. The modern mass-market paperback romance novel we know and love today came out during the sexual revolution of the 1970s.

After hundreds of years of restrictions on female sexuality, women were finally able to start exploring their own desires, thanks to bigger social trends from changing perceptions of a woman's role to the invention and widespread use of the birth control pill.

The modern romance industry was born in 1972 with the publication of *The Flame and the Flower* by Kathleen E. Woodiwiss, at a time when even *Cosmopolitan* magazine declared in a feature article that, "Women do not have sexual fantasies, period. Men do."[18]

It was, admittedly, a troubling start for the modern reader: In that epic, historical novel set at the turn of the nineteenth century, the hero mistakes the heroine for a prostitute (not that this should matter) and rapes her. Their forced marriage is the beginning of their grand romance, and this book is the beginning of the erotic romance that doesn't shy away from depicting sex as an important part of a satisfying relationship.

After centuries of being told that lust in women needed to be controlled or conversely that their gender was "not troubled by sexual feelings of any kind," women found that their sexual feelings could be a mystery, even to themselves. Romance novels changed the conversation. Yes, women had sexual desires. Yes, women experienced sexual pleasure. Romance novels came to provide a safe place for women to explore their desires, free from the risk of rape, guilt, judgment, slut-shaming, disease, unplanned pregnancy, or regret. In contrast to so many other depictions of sex, from literature to porn to movies, romance novels are completely and unabashedly focused on the woman's feelings and pleasure. And, most revolutionarily of all, romance heroines can enjoy sex and still live happily ever after.

#6 Because HEA

> *Decide what makes you happy and damn what anyone else*
> *thinks or says.*
> —*Rush* by Maya Banks

If a fictional heroine escapes the confines of the house, chooses love, has orgasmic sex, and dies at the end of the story, the message is clear: Don't try this at home. But if she lives happily ever after? The message is also clear: Live the dream, girl!

In romance novels, the heroine lives. Not only that, she lives happily ever after, which is shorthand for a life of being loved for oneself and for having achieved a measure of security.

But the happy ending is about more than marriage and more than love. There is social acceptance of the romantic couple, showing that two individuals can push boundaries and still be accepted by society and perhaps even change it. Good people are rewarded. Bad people are punished. There is, quite simply, emotional justice. It is implied that the couple will have a measure of financial security. Often, they welcome babies, showing that mother and baby have lived through childbirth (a real danger for most of human history) and that there is a new generation, born and raised with love. Above all, there is hope for the future that is more loving and accepting of a greater variety of people.

The happy ending also makes the reader happy. There is a certain feeling when one has just finished a good romance, and you're basking in that happily-ever-after glow—you want to feel that again. So the lady readers seeks more books, the lady authors write more books, and publishers are financially incentivized to churn out more and more and more books declaring that women are worth it and that they deserve autonomy, pleasure, and love. More and more women come to believe that they deserve a good story—on the page, and in real life.

Viva la romance revolution.

THREE

PROOF OF SNARK

EVIDENCE OF ROMANCE'S BAD REPUTATION

IF I HAD any doubt that the romance genre had a bad reputation, the survey data confirmed it. People who took my survey for non-romance readers and had admittedly not read the genre offered the following descriptions: "Fluff reading, for not very bright individuals"; "Formulaic and generally mediocre writing"; "Unrealistic. Lesser quality writing and vocabulary"; "Not addressing the larger issues in life. Dependence upon detailed sex scenes which can be too stereotypically he-mannish."

They described the readers as "stuck in a rut," "sorority girls or bored housewives," and "romantics, people who like their comfort zone, not very original perhaps?" And those were just the first few responses. Overall survey respondents thought romance readers were less educated and had a lower income than they actually do.

Romance readers are well aware of how they and their beloved books are perceived. Eighty-five percent of readers feel that romance novels have a bad reputation and 89 percent also believe that romance readers were looked down upon.

Half of readers felt they should keep their romance reading a secret. "I definitely had the conception of dedicated romance readers as cat ladies," says Jenn Northington, the former event manager at WORD Bookstore in Brooklyn, New York. That is, before she started reading them, meeting the readers, and eventually becoming a romance fan herself.

The truth is, there is a huge variety of romance novels and readers, but still, the stereotypes remain. "It's just out there in the ether," says Courtney Milan, a bestselling author of historical romance. It certainly appeared to be so, but I wanted to find proof of the snark. I found examples in the way we talk about romance novels, but it's most apparent in how and where we do *not* talk about romance novels, such as the book review sections of prestigious publications, academic institutions, or even the dictionary.

A romance by any other name

The Urban Dictionary defines a romance novel as "literary porn," which in its own way is flattering in that it is a rare instance of acknowledging romance as *literary*. Also, porn, by their definition, is "The best thing in the world." However, indicative of contrasting views, the second definition is "garbage."

At least the Urban Dictionary actually offers a definition of *romance novel*. Look up *romance novel* in any other dictionary and you'll be surprised at what you don't find. Dictionary.com can't find it. Merriam-Webster.com wonders if you meant "roman numeral."

All of these dictionaries do offer standard definitions of "science fiction" and "comic book," revealing that it's not an issue with genre fiction overall, but a very specific type of

genre fiction. However, Dictionary.com does offer a definition of "mommy porn":

> **noun, informal.** *1. sexually explicit or porno-*
> *graphic books, photos, videos, etc., that*
> *appeal to women, especially middle-aged*
> *women. British: mummy porn.*

Ugh.

If you look up just *romance,* the results go something like
this:

> **noun (1):** *a medieval tale based on legend,*
> *chivalric love and adventure, or the super-*
> *natural (2): a prose narrative treating*
> *imaginary characters involved in events*
> *remote in time or place and usually heroic,*
> *adventurous, or mysterious (3): a love*
> *story especially in the form of a novel*

They offer the classical definitions. But they also *don't*
say the same thing: They don't offer anything remotely
resembling the way millions of readers understand the genre
to be today or come close to the official definition from
Romance Writers of America (RWA):

A central love story: The main plot centers around individuals falling in love and struggling to make the relationship
work. A writer can include as many subplots as he/she wants
as long as the love story is the main focus of the novel.

An emotionally satisfying and optimistic ending: In a
romance, the lovers who risk and struggle for each other and
their relationship are rewarded with emotional justice and
unconditional love.

But if one were to look up *romance novel* in the *Oxford English Dictionary of Literary Terms*, a little book of required reading for university students in English departments, they would not find the term. Of course, science fiction and fantasy have a full page dedicated to each of them.

I would like to see these dictionaries include a definition of *romance novel* that would be recognizable to millions of contemporary readers today. When *non-romance* readers were asked how they would define a romance novel, they hit the highlights of the RWA definition:

- "Girl meets boy/woman meets man, a few problems here and there but they manage to surmount them and voilà! happy ending."
- "A story that features a couple getting together, being separated by evil relatives or innocent misunderstandings, then reuniting at the end."
- "The romantic relationship is the main plot."
- "Boy meets girl, fall in love, have sexual encounters, maybe a little problem or dramatic heartache/death something, but then somehow everything works out and they find love at the end."

If even non-romance readers have the same understanding of this term *romance novel*, it appears that we're all operating with a similar definition of what it means.

In recent years, selfie, bling, and dance-off were added to the Oxford English Dictionary. The Oxford Dictionary Online saw the addition of squee, twerk, and jorts. It's time to include *romance novel* as we know it.

Bodice rippers in the media

For a long time the mainstream media mostly ignored the romance industry. There weren't many reviews of the books, profiles of the authors, or discussions of trends in the genre. But occasionally, romance finds itself in the headlines of traditional media outlets and it's often easy to see the snark.

When HarperCollins (owned by NewsCorp) bought romance publisher Harlequin for $415 million, it was big business and publishing news. At a time when the publishing industry is in flux and the "Big 6" are consolidating, it's a big deal when one massive publisher acquires another. Even for a serious business article, *The New York Times* used the headline "Bodice Ripper in New Hands[1]." (even though the term bodice ripper technically never really applied to Harlequin romances).

The first few paragraphs were wisecracks. There was the inevitable Fabio mention ("The very word Harlequin conjures images of shirtless hunks—Fabio Lanzoni was a famous cover model in the 1980s and '90s—and lusty women."). In contrast, when Penguin and Random House merged, the headline was a staid "Penguin and Random House Will Merge, Saying Change Will Come Slowly[2]" to match the straightforward text of the article: "Together, Penguin and Random House will make up the biggest and most dominant publisher in the business." Yawn. But accurate. And snark-free.

When *The New York Times* does talk about romance novels, the results are widespread, long-lasting, and cringe-inducing. They're credited with popularizing the terms *bodice ripper* and *mommy porn*. Both phrases diminish the genre by reducing it to just "the naughty bits" and insult the reader by implying that they're reading smut. But at least romance is being talked about?

When *Harper's* magazine published an article on the genre, "Bad romance: One genre and a billion happy endings," [3] the author went to great lengths to position the genre poorly by juxtaposing the story of aspiring writers, self-published successes, and hunky cover models at a romance conference with a news story about a man who killed his friend's wife, son, and dog, torched their house, and kidnapped the daughter. It's not clear what the author was trying to accomplish—perhaps to highlight the stark contrast between the happy endings in books and real-life tragedies on the news? Romance authors are worried about selling their happy books when really, love is fucked up and people go crazy and die?

In other instances, the lack of mentions of romance novels is shocking. In 2014, the *Atlantic* published an article entitled "Why Is It So Hard for Women to Write about Sex?"[4] It doesn't even mention the billion dollar industry of women writing happily about sex. The subtitle of the article is "Because it's easier to titillate, shock, and lie than to get at the messy truth about female desire." Of course, this is something the romance genre has been doing explicitly for decades. In 2013, *The New York Times* did a feature called "Let's Read about Sex"[5] and neglected to include the perspective of *any* romance author. They at least published a Letter to the Editor from bestselling romance author Sarah MacLean, who wrote "I was dismayed to see that of the 15 authors asked to discuss writing about sex in the 'Naughty Bits' roundup, none write romance novels—the genre best known for its naughty bits."[6]

This all changed with the phenomenon of *Fifty Shades of Grey*. When it was "discovered" by non-romance readers, suddenly this book became too popular to ignore. In a deluge of blog posts and articles, people declared this book the death of feminism and a cause of abusive relationships and criticized the entire genre ("Romance novels, like racists, tend to be the same wherever you turn," writes William Giraldi, in a scathing piece for the *New Republic*[7]).

But the romance lovers had a response for all those haters, and they took to their blogs to defend the genre. Some mainstream media even published articles that reported more favorably on romance. For example, the *Atlantic* published "Beyond Bodice Rippers: How Romance Novels Came to Embrace Feminism[8]," which examines how authors are writing more empowered heroines, especially when it comes to sex. On their website, NPR published an article entitled "Don't Hide Your Harlequins: In Defense of Romance[9]" about a romance reader overcoming the sense of shame she was made to feel for her reading material.

Entertainment Weekly featured a multi-page story about the romance genre, including graphics, in their October 2014 issue, which was widely regarded as fair and favorable. Some comments from the romance blog at *USA Today* were about what was awesome in the *Entertainment Weekly* article: that the author interviewed prominent authors (not obscure ones) to represent the genre, she attended the annual Romance Writers of America conference (the "right" one to go to), she didn't take a condescending tone, and she reported on romance's great numbers (the billion-dollar industry, the millions of readers, etc).

Whether the angle is favorable or scathing, there is at least a conversation about the genre, its values, and what it means about the everyday lives of real people. Finally.

Romance novels: available wherever drugs are sold!

A 2009 Time magazine featured an article on the genre. This is how it began:

> Romance novels, an inexpensive escape for women, are helping some publishers hide from the worst of the recession. Frequently an impulse purchase, mass-market paperback romances, often bought on the run at drugstores and supermarkets, cost $4.75 to $5.99—a bargain when hardcover editions are typically $25 or more.[10]

The snark packed into the paragraph is marvelous—but presumably not done maliciously by author, as she is simply echoing popular perceptions. First, these novels are immediately and repeatedly classified as cheap—both in terms of price point and in comparison to other offerings on the market, like hardcover books and the sort of books that appear in hardcover (most often nonfiction or literary fiction).

There is also the implication that they are substandard literature, not simply because of the low price but because frequently they are *not even purchased from a bookstore.* Where romances are sold may be part of the reason they are considered low-brow, crappy lit.

Until recently, bookstores have been the largest source for romance buying, and the mass-market paperback was the format of choice. Though there is a long history of developments leading up to it, Robert DeGraff , a founder of Pocket Books, is credited with creating the widespread distribution of mass-market paperbacks, which contributed to the massive growth of the romance industry. He was "aware of a relative lack of bookstores in the United States and of the general population's feeling that those establishments were intimidating and inhospitable, and concluded that books would have to be marketed somewhere else if they were to be sold on a grand scale."[11] That somewhere else was drugstores and grocery stores, and DeGraff used magazine distributors to get the books out. They were priced at "a mere 25 cents."[12] Not only were these books cheap and not sold in bookstores, but also the audience was (or perceived to be) intimidated by serious hardcovers and bookstores.

Harlequin built on this to enormous success by putting their products into retail outlets where their customers, women, frequently shopped: grocery stores and drugstores. "Harlequin pioneered paperback sales in supermarkets across the continent...Once this started to take off, the growth of Harlequin became exponential."[13] A woman could purchase a romance novel (or more) and disguise it as part of her grocery budget from a husband who presumably wouldn't condone spending on such trashy books.

In the 1970s, Harlequin built their business and readership by giving out free romance novels in Kotex boxes (yes, sales for the sanitary pads increased), Ajax cleanser, laundry detergent, and cosmetics and even at McDonald's one Mother's Day. [14] While these tactics built their brand, they also associated romance with things that are "shameful," dirty, need to be covered up, or cheap, unhealthy junk food.

In fact, cheap fiction and drugstores have an even longer history together. In his book, *The Reading Nation in the Romantic Period,* William St Clair writes about the rural English communities that relied on chapmen (also called walking stationers, peddlers, hawkers, and "mercuries") to distribute books and supply "scissors, ribbons, perfumes, medicines, and other small manufactured goods which were not made locally," all of which sounds like the stuff you'd find at a drugstore today. "Indeed, the alliance between books and pharmaceuticals, industries that shared many economic characteristics, operated continuously from the age of the manuscript to the twentieth century."[15]

Because these men carried their wares on their backs, they often offered small books such as ballads and chapbooks for purchase. St Clair points out that "the popular rural market was therefore concentrated on the lower tranches of print which included abridgments and books sold in parts or serially in 'numbers.'" The link between lightweight, cheap books and less educated rural readers predates stereotypes about drugstore books in flyover states.

The association of drugstores and grocery stores with romance novels helped create certain associations: These are addictive books (available wherever drugs are sold), purchased by love-starved women (of course a love-starved women would fill up with a love story from the supermarket). And by extension, it has driven unflattering stereotypes about the romance reader.

One of the biggest retail outlets today for print romance novels are mass merchandise retailers like Walmart, Target, Costco, and so on. These stores are known for their massive quantities of cheaply made products; their whole mission is to have the lowest price and the cheapest stuff money can buy. Stores like these and how they advertise have fetishized cheap. The customers, whether in truth or not, also don't have the best reputation (ahem, the cruel www.peopleofwalmart.-com). And this is where romance novels are sold in huge quantities. It's guilt by association (even if it's not something to feel guilty about).

As with drugstores, the mass merchandise retailers are also stores where people don't deliberately go to buy books, which means that romances are likely to be impulse purchases, as the *Time* article describes. It's true that 27 percent of romance novel purchases are impulse buys and 30 percent of purchasers planned to buy a book but not the specific one they walked out of the store with.[16]

Romance readers and impulse seem to go hand in hand and that suggests a lack of forethought, planning, or anticipation on the part of the purchaser. The implication with all this "impulsive" reading is that the reader of romance cannot control their passions and desires—a long-held fear about women. The lack of thought and reason implied in an impulse purchase also drives home the association that these are not thought-provoking books; they're dumb, cheap crap you buy in a hurry, read quickly, and throw away.

By 2012, supermarkets and grocery stores accounted for just 3 percent of romance sales. Mass merchandisers accounted for 17 percent, bookstores for 9 percent, and a whopping 46 percent of romance novels were purchased online.[17]

When romance novels are sold in bookstores, they are often found in chains like Barnes & Noble or the late Borders and Waldenbooks. These stores are commonly found in shopping malls and strip malls, places for the masses to shop. Now, of course, we all bemoan the disappearance of the bookstore, even if it was in the mall.

When I asked non-romance readers where they saw romance novels for sale, independent bookstores ranked lowest. Way down low. Indeed, Bowker Market Research shows that in 2012, independent bookstores had only 2 percent of the romance market share.[18] Independent bookstores, of course, are where the smart, literary books are hand-sold by intellectual booksellers—or at least that is the perception. They are individual, unique, quirky; they are not mass. They are not where you expect romances to be sold, and often they aren't.

That's not to say that all independent bookstores ignore a "low-brow" but lucrative fiction. WORD Brooklyn is an independent bookstore in hipster central, and they carry romance novels after working with a local romance author and publisher to develop and curate their selection. But for many buyers at independent bookstores, it's not just a snobby attitude that keeps these books off the shelves: Some just don't know where to start when it comes to stocking romance since it's outside of their expertise or reading interest. At least, that's the perception of Jenn Northington, the former event manager at WORD, whom I spoke to on the phone about independent bookstores and romance. "Some are being snooty. But I don't think that's the whole story. It's very easy to feel lost and not know what on earth you should focus on," she says. "It's a specialized knowledge base most people don't have access to."

Because WORD is a tiny shop, there is no dedicated romance section; instead romance novels are shelved with all the other fiction. Literary fiction, romance, mysteries, and sci-fi are all together on the shelf. "Once we started carrying romance and talking actively about it, we noticed a lot of women—usually professionals or grad students—would grab them in addition to picking up the new Meg Wolitzer or Donna Tartt," Northington says. "They wanted reading that was going to engage them but also be entertaining and a break from their work. Once we made it acceptable inside the store confines to read all of those things at the same time, they did." Placement plays a huge role in how romance is represented and what messages are sent about its quality and readership, and in this instance we see how simple placement can give "permission" to read the books without it being a disparaging statement on one's intellect.

Shelf placement can also have a profound impact on the

visibility and success of a book or genre, as we see when it comes to romances featuring diverse characters. In a typical large bookstore, romance novels featuring, say, black characters might be shelved in the section devoted to African American Studies, even though its readers are more likely to be found browsing the romance section for a fun novel to take on vacation. For a reader craving a pirate romance, she might not care if the pirate is black, white, gay, straight, or whatever, as long as there's a love story that ends happily. But if she can't find it, she can't buy it.

Separate sections can give the impression that certain types of subgenres of romance "don't sell" when in fact they just aren't placed where their audience is looking for them. This can lead to a vicious cycle where authors avoid writing these books and publishers avoid bringing them to market, even though there's a readership hungry for them. As a result, interested readers might be prevented from finding books easily that they might enjoy, whether it's an interracial romance or just a romance novel at all—even if, or especially if, it's not something they might deliberately seek out.

It's worth it for an independent bookseller to incorporate romance. Women are the biggest book buyers: They purchase 65 percent of books and account for 58 percent of dollars spent. A typical book buyer—a woman, with an average age of 41, a college degree, and income of 50,000 or higher—looks a lot like the demographics for the romance buyer.[19] Northington points out that they'll sell more books at romance events than ones featuring books and authors of other genres. "People who come to a romance event come prepared to buy books." In an age when independent bookstores are facing constant pressures to survive, WORD in Brooklyn has opened a second location.

It's impossible to talk about selling books without

mentioning Amazon. While it started as an online bookstore, it is now, like Walmart, a place where you can buy diapers, tampons, drugs, and...a 99-cent romance novel. Between the company these books keep on the virtual shelves and with that oh-so-easy one-click purchase button, the association of romance novels as cheap, impulsively purchased commodities is only reinforced further.

While it may not help romance's reputation, there are some real bonuses to being sold in a wide variety of retailers. For one thing, they're available in a wide variety of retailers. As we see stores come (Amazon, iBooks, Smashwords, Scribd, Oyster Books, etc.) and go (Borders, Waldenbooks, various independents), the romance industry has adapted to new vendors and largely kept up their stellar sales even when some outlets have gone bust. That's not to say the publishing industry hasn't taken some major hits to their sales and bottom lines by the loss of some traditional outlets, but having books available in many places means more books can be sold. For authors, having more books out there creates more chances to build a readership that will follow you from book to book...or retailer to retailer.

One of the most profound effects of being so cheap and sold in a wide variety of retailers is that romance novels are readily available to people who wouldn't otherwise have access to a library or bookstore—or who cannot afford a $25 hardcover. This is a GREAT thing. Everyone deserves affordable and uplifting entertainment. Everyone deserves the opportunity to have access to books and the education they provide, even if it's "just" improved language and reading skills (which are more likely to be developed if one has something entertaining and fun to read). But then again, that's what they were afraid of, isn't it?

What does a girl have to do to get her book reviewed around here?

Nora Roberts (and her alter ego J. D. Robb) has written more than 214 books and more than 191 them have been *New York Times* bestsellers. Nora's books have spent a combined 198 weeks at the number one spot on the bestseller list (which adds up to 3.5 years) and 58 books debuted at #1. These numbers are the latest available as of this writing and the numbers are going higher by the minute.[20]

She has had only two *New York Times* book reviews of her work.

Jennifer Weiner, a bestselling author and advocate for the equal representation of women's fiction, has noticed that this isn't just limited to Nora Roberts; there is a lack of reviews in prestigious publications for authors of all types of women's commercial fiction. Or even just writers who happen to have vaginas. Weiner makes a point to shed light on this discrepancy and advocate for more attention to women's fiction. She also gets to the heart of why it matters: "Declining to cover the books that women read is another way of making women invisible—women writers, women readers. It silences voices, erases an audience, sends the message that women's stories don't matter (or matter only enough to show up in the Style section)."[21]

An organization of women in literary arts, VIDA, keeps count of gender balance (or imbalances) at major media publications. In 2013 (the last year numbers are available), *The New York Times* reviewed 482 male authors and 332 female authors. But we shouldn't just keep picking on *The New York Times* just because they happen to be the most visible and prestigious publication. *The Atlantic*, which has a robust "Sexes" section and has published some amazing articles on the women's experience, reviewed 3 female authors and 17 male authors. VIDA has more data for a variety of publications available, and the numbers show that overall more men get their work reviewed as well as do the reviewing. And this isn't just about romance; it's about the uphill battles women authors face, even when they're writing in more critically respectable genres. In this very competitive environment, romance doesn't stand a chance.

Even publications that seem to have an audience that would love to read reviews of romance novels shy away from it. Two come to mind: *Oprah* and *People*. Both cover mainstream women's fiction, but it's very rare to see a mass-market paperback get a review in either of these publications.

In the absence of Respectable Reviews from Established Publications, there has been an explosion of blogs devoted to romance book reviews. There are big, established ones like Dear Author, Smart Bitches, Trashy Books, Heroes & Heartbreakers, or Happy Ever After, the blog from *USA Today*. There are hundreds, if not thousands, of smaller blogs with their own communities.

It makes sense for romance authors to promote their books and seek reviews from places that serve an audience of devoted romance readers. Why should an author even bother pitching to the big media that probably wouldn't feature the book anyway? For example, it might not make sense for an individual romance author to pitch *People* magazine on the third novel in their six-book series, if it's not already a bestseller. But the result of shying away from pitching to the biggies is that those editors aren't receiving a significant number of pitches from romance authors that would make them sit up and say, "Hey, there's a big audience here" or "Hey, I think I spot a trend!"

And when romance authors talk just among ourselves,

we're not engaging with new-to-romance readers and bringing them into the fold or showing a different side of the genre than the tired stereotypes.

It can be argued that if readers are able to find reviews of books they want to read, why does it matter *where* those reviews are posted? "I know there's a part of the feminist world that is like, 'Hey, screw 'em, we'll do our own thing over here,' and I can see there's a value in that," says Erin Belieu, cofounder of VIDA, in an interview with *Mother Jones*. "But a kind of nudgy part of me thinks: No. I want access, and I want my daughters to have access to the exact same thing, because we all know there's no such thing as separate but equal." [22]

When an independent bookstore puts romance on the shelf with all the other fiction, the association declares, "It's all okay! Happy reading!" In contrast, a significant lack of regular reviews of an entire genre of fiction—and the largest segment of fiction, which is the largest segment of books sold —declares that these works and these readers are not worthy of participation in bigger cultural conversations. And these books should be included: "Genre fiction is a great way to comment on the world without being too on the nose," points out Petra Mayer, an editor at NPR Books, who has championed coverage of romance there. Excluding women's fiction suggests that women's interests aren't worthy of discussion and that women's voices don't deserve to be heard. "In terms of combating pervasive institutional bias around stories around women—that would be why I want to fight for romance to have a wider audience," says Mayer.

A lack of substantial reviews of women's fiction also makes a subtle statement about who these publications think their audience is, which ends up reinforcing the stereotype of the stupid book, stupid reader. Jane Litte, founder of the blog

Dear Author notes, "When you review, you're starting a conversation about the book. When you publicly review, you're starting a conversation about the book with people you perceive as your intended audience." To be fair, perhaps romance readers *aren't* the audience of the *Paris Review* or *The New York Times*. But is that because they don't find coverage of books they're interested in reading, so they don't bother to read *The New York Times*? Mayer points out that NPR has done audience research that shows they do want to see reviews of science fiction, fantasy, and a little bit of romance.

I imagine that many romance readers are not reading *The New York Times Book Review*, but I also bet there are a fair number of smart, intellectual romance readers that are, and they have gotten the message that one type of book they enjoy reading is not "fit for print," so they don't speak publicly about it. Again, this only reinforces the stigma.

Of course, the genre as a whole is doing just fine without mainstream attention, and prestigious book reviews will hardly make or break Nora Roberts' career. If readers want reviews of romance novels, they can turn to Amazon pages or any one of the thousands of blogs devoted to romance reviews. "The only reason you need mainstream criticism is just to improve the quality of work so people know what's good," Mayer says. And, I would add, so new readers easily learn what's good and feel that it's acceptable to read it.

In the past year, things have started to change. NPR now includes coverage of romance novels. *The Washington Post* features a monthly column of romance book reviews, penned by romance author Sarah Maclean. *USA Today* does have an online blog solely devoted to romance. *The New York Times* has published op-eds in defense of romance from bestselling authors Eloisa James and Sarah Maclean. But this coverage is still collected together and kept separate in a way that other books aren't. Romance can be covered en masse as part of a Valentine's Day theme or in a separate column, but it's still rare to see a full-fledged, standalone review of one romance novel.

Romance in academia

In a notable media appearance for the genre in July 2009, *USA Today* ran an article entitled "Scholarly writers empower the romance genre."[23] That scholars are romance authors is considered a newsworthy angle says it all—it's unlikely that one would see an article entitled "Scholarly writers empower literary fiction." The article even begins, "Thirty years ago, 'Ivy League romance writer' was like 'jumbo shrimp'—an oxymoron." This isn't necessarily true, and there are a lot of other potentially contributing factors about women's roles and education thirty years earlier (in 1979!). The point is that the popular perception of romance readers and authors is that they are uneducated at best or just plain stupid. It's not true.

In my survey of non-romance readers, I asked them to select what they thought was highest level of education achieved by most romance readers. Only 8 percent thought a master's degree; 37 percent believed it to be a bachelor's, and the rest thought they had accomplished some high school (or none) or an associate's degree. In my study of romance readers, 66 percent had achieved a bachelor's degree or higher. This is not perfect methodology by any means, but it shows that non-romance readers generally believe romance readers to have less education than they do—and presumably they are less intellectual or just plain dumb as well.

When questions of education and romance come up, people love to point to Eloisa James (Harvard/Yale/Oxford),

Julia Quinn (Harvard/Yale), Stephanie Laurens (PhD in biochemistry), Lauren Willig (Yale/Harvard Law), or countless others. But what matters isn't necessarily how many readers have advance degrees or how many romance authors went to the Ivy Leagues.

What matters is the academic study of the romance genre. "It's been institutionalized as anti-intellectual," says Bobbi Dumas, the founder of Read a Romance Month. It's due in part to the lack of formal academic attention to the genre. This sends the message that it's not worthy of study or that there is nothing about it to study.

When I was an undergraduate at New York University studying women's role in fiction, both as writers and characters, it was my mother—not one of my professors—who insisted that I include romance novels, "the most popular and profitable books by women for women." After she went to great lengths to convince me to read one, I then had to convince my professors to allow me to include these books in my independent studies, because there was no course on romance novels. The closest was a class on love in literature, which devoted more time to reading and discussing the sob fest *The Sorrows of Young Werther* than romance novels; half a class was spent on an excerpt from Janice Radway's hate-read classic *Reading the Romance: Women, Patriarchy, and Popular Literature,* which hardly portrays popular romance in a flattering light (and which has since had its methodology questioned by other scholars).

Romance is largely absent from the school curriculum, and not just in my own experience. Forty-six percent of survey respondents said it was covered in school, but digging deeper, I discovered that the main works covered were *Pride and Prejudice* and *Jane Eyre,* which have become acceptable as literature, not as romance.

Yet, it's not impossible to get romance covered in academia—a student often just needs to ask. My professors weren't hostile when I approached them about including romance novels in my thesis—in fact, they were curious and open. But then a new set of problems presents itself: a current lack of scholarship on the genre to study. Jennifer Probst, a bestselling contemporary romance novelist, describes her experience writing her master's thesis on happy endings: "I think I found maybe one really good journal article," she told me. There are some academic books on romance, but they're limited in scope. "They're analyzing Harlequin," Probst says. "This is nothing against Harlequin. They're judging an entire industry on Harlequin romance novels, and let's just be honest, that's just a small segment."

Professor Pamela Regis notes the same flaw in research on the genre: "These authors of three of the founding texts in the criticism of the romance novel all generalize hastily."[24] Many critics focus exclusively on a small subset of the genre —Radway focuses just on the long historical novels of the 1970s, and Tania Modleski cites just nine Harlequin titles— and many draw conclusions based on the whole of the romance genre after reading only a handful of books.

Similarly, as I was doing research for this book, I was hard pressed to find books about the genre that were recently published—most dated from the 1980s and 1990s. Given how quickly and significantly the genre can change, I see this as a major problem.

However, this is starting to change. Dr. Sarah Frantz Lyons, editorial director with RipTide publishing and a "recovering academic," teamed up with scholar Eric Selinger to create the International Association for the Study of Popular Romance to promote studies on the genre and legitimize it as a field of study.

"What we were trying to do with our association, conferences, and journals is to establish a background that grad students could then take to committees and programs to say 'look there is this body of scholars studying this,'" she says. "That gives them legitimacy to propose a dissertation about popular romance fiction because there is a body of work behind them." This means more journal articles and other works for scholars to draw from—and hopefully more and more professors will incorporate romance into regular curriculum, if not offer specialized classes in it.

The romance in academia movement is growing, and it's being driven by organizations like the International Association for the Study of Popular Romance and professors like Pamela Regis, an English professor at McDaniel College in Westminster, Maryland. She also directs the Nora Roberts Center for American Romance at McDaniel, which offers a degree program in writing romance novels—something you'd be hard-pressed to find included in most MFA programs.

Other universities aren't shying away from romance. In 2009, Princeton University—that posh Ivy League institution —hosted an academic conference entitled "Love as the Practice of Freedom? Romance Fiction and American Culture." It's a significant step for the genre, which, as you might expect, hasn't gotten a lot of class time or office hours devoted to it. "When I saw the invitation to speak at Princeton, I said, "Holy crap, we have arrived,'" says Regis.[25]

While romance novels should be included in the scholarly conversation, we also need to be aware of how we talk about them—and it can't be defensively, Frantz Lyons points out. In fact, it all has to operate on the "fundamental belief that romance is worth studying." Think about it: Most works on the genre start out justifying it as a field of study by quoting the numbers (a billion dollars, a million readers, etc.). But

Frantz Lyons points out how limiting that can be, even
though it's well intentioned: "We got a whole bunch of new
ways of thinking about romance when you aren't spending a
quarter of your article trying to defend the fact that this is
what you are studying to begin with."

As romance becomes more accepted in academia—thanks
to pioneering professors, scholars, and determined students—
it will be interesting to see how the perception of the genre
changes once it's studied alongside the traditional canon.
Notable Ivy League romance writer and Shakespeare
professor Eloisa James says, "I think that romance is in a
sense being rehabilitated by young women scholars who are
studying the genre. Mystery really rehabbed when it moved
into the college curriculum. Romance is in the curriculum
now, too." Before long, it might just be in the mainstream.

Coming out at cocktail parties

One of the best perks about writing romance novels is that
you almost always have the coolest job at a party—that is, if
you dare to mention it when people ask what you do. I always
answer truthfully and only once did I get the pinched face of
disapproval (from a very done-up middle-aged woman at my
grandmother's country club). Usually, people—and women
especially—are *fascinated,* and I'm not alone in getting this
reaction.

Tessa Woodward, a senior editor at Avon (and my
romance editor!), describes how the genders react differently
when she tells people what she does: "I get a lot of guys who
just want to talk about it. It's the most fascinating thing
they've ever heard of. And then I get a lot of women who just
sit there, and then later they corner me to say 'Okay, so
secretly I love romance. What do you recommend?'"

DANGEROUS BOOKS FOR GIRLS

Kensington romance editor Esi Sogah has noticed a similar pattern of conversations when she tells people what she does for a living: "After the first 30 seconds of skepticism and jokes, people get really, really interested. Like genuinely curious and surprised when I tell them various writers' backgrounds and vast variety of books out there. And I have converted many a friend to a happy romance reader."

Have readers so internalized the idea that they should be ashamed of reading romance that they don't dare mention it in polite company? In my survey, half of readers report feeling like they should keep their romance reading a secret. When asked if they're "out" with regards to their reading material, most said yes, but a significant number, 36 percent, said "only with certain people." And 85 percent of readers think the genre has a bad reputation. No wonder people can be reluctant to bring it up in a group of strangers.

The world may not actually be as snarky toward romance as readers of the genre perceive it to be. But by assuming we'll get a certain reaction (jokes about bodice rippers, trashy books, and Fabio!) and trying to avoid it by keeping silent, romance lovers are missing an opportunity to engage people in conversation—and perhaps start changing the perception of the genre.

Sogah often sees readers keep quiet about it until they realize they're in a like-minded group. "I'm assuming you think this is a bad thing so I'll go along with it until told otherwise," she summarizes. Or if romance reading is mentioned, it is done so in the same breath as more prestigious works. It's like "Before you can criticize me...I was reading Voltaire yesterday," Sogah says. This dynamic of keeping silent until it is "safe" suggests that romance readers are aware that their reading material is considered something to be ashamed of. It also shows that we can be defensive about it—or just plain weary of *having* to defend it and explain it to people. Who really wants to combat the snark at a party?

But Sogah points out something that echoes my own experiences—people may ask about "trashy books" or "bodice rippers" but "it's not said in a way that's meant to be insulting. They're not offended by romance novel's existence. I would say those same people generally have no real exposure to romance novels."

FOUR

TRASHY BOOKS

IT'S hard to avoid the phrase "trashy books" when talking about romance novels. To be fair, other mass media like tabloid magazines and reality TV are often deemed trashy entertainment. But this disparagement seems to be somewhat affectionate and is tempered with a mention of guilty pleasures ("Trashy books are my guilty pleasure.") We tend to understand this as a judgment on the quality of the content, but how these books are produced contributes significantly to the perception of these books as somehow substandard.

When it comes to the romance industry, much of what has made it so successful (read: profitable) is exactly what condemns it to the pile of cheap, trashy books. When romance novels are created, manufactured, marketed, and distributed, they are cheaply produced and cheaply sold in large quantities. Traditional ways of conferring value to a product such as expense, craftsmanship, or exclusivity are not relevant when it comes to the physical or digital production of romance novels. For better or worse, romance novels exemplify commodity literature.

A tale of two books

When comparing a typical mass-market paperback and a hardcover book, the difference in the physical quality of the product is immediately apparent. One has a solid, durable cover, perhaps wrapped in a glossy dust jacket, with high quality paper pages inside. One has a cover that's only a little thicker than the lightweight paper the contents are printed on. A hardcover looks and feels like it's built to last, while a mass-market paperback feels like you could chuck it in the recycling with the daily newspaper.

"How many romance authors end up in hardcover?" asks bestselling author Courtney Milan. "Fewer than in any other genre."

Hardcovers are, of course, more expensive. To make money on cheap books like mass-market paperbacks, the romance industry relies on volume. This requires authors to churn out manuscripts for readers to voraciously devour. While approximately 30 percent of Americans read between one and five books[1] a year, 35 percent of romance readers read more than five books a week. The esteemed and celebrated author of the novel *The Art of Fielding*, took ten years to write that one book. Nora Roberts publishes an average of six books per year.

Just because they are written relatively quickly and cheaply produced doesn't mean they aren't beloved. Some of the most popular cheap books in earlier centuries were literally read to pieces as they were passed from reader to reader. The inexpensive cardboard covers and low quality paper literally disintegrated from being read so much. But it's the hardcovers, made with quality and preserved on the library shelf, that are more likely to have survived through the ages.

Judging a book by its packaging

"There's a certain commoditization of romance that you don't see in other genres," says Jane Litte, of the popular blog Dear Author. Let's face it: The books are largely and reliably the same. To an extent, we see this in the content but it's especially clear in the physical book. Most are published in the small, lightweight mass-market paperback format and bear strikingly similar covers and titles. It's not a coincidence that they all look so alike; it's the most effective way to produce and market a large number of books to a particular audience.

This is true now and it was true in the eighteenth and nineteenth centuries, too. The commoditization of literature was a deliberate attempt to maximize profits and minimize risk. It was achieved by standardizing the physical product and the content of the stories, the audience to whom they were targeted, and marketing efforts based on the book's similarities rather than their uniqueness. They're all interconnected.

It starts with paper in the eighteenth and nineteenth centuries

Paper was expensive, and it was made by hand from old cloth, often picked off dead bodies on European battlefields.[2] In England, paper was also heavily taxed and those regulations prevented the supply of paper in quantities of less than half a ream (a ream equals approximately 516 pages).

Publishers based their edition sizes on their raw materials, particularly paper. In his exhaustively detailed book *The Reading Nation in the Romantic Period,* William St Clair writes that "since publishers had to estimate the amount of paper needed for an edition to the nearest half ream, they sometimes asked authors to lengthen or shorten the text, or to add smaller pieces to bulk out a volume as late as the proof stage."[3] Sometimes publishers wouldn't even ask the author; they would just stop when they ran out of paper, sometimes letting books end in midsentence!

But when authors are funding the publication of their work, whether in the eighteenth century or twenty-first, they exert "almost total control over their works, which were then conceived as the unique products of their own individual intellects," writes Janice Radway.[4] This shows the tensions between the romantic era idea of art as divinely inspired and the practicalities of making a product for profit. Presumably you don't amend or silence an artistic truth for something as banal as the cost of paper.

But publishers did have to account for the cost of paper, taxes, and the number of copies they could reasonably expect to sell. Not only did they have to conform to the tax laws, but in order to generate a profit, they had to make efficient use of the resources available. Paper was expensive and a publisher could not afford to waste it. An author could not afford to anger the publisher by refusing to comply—and to what point? There was only so much paper—and plenty of aspiring authors. So stories were cut or lengthened on demand. Artistic truth answered to the demands of the market, and this was a repellent idea to some people. One nineteenth century author writes disparagingly of this cheap literature:

No divine influence can be imagined as presiding over the birth of his work, beyond the market-law of demand and supply; no more immortality is dreamed of for it than for the fashions of the current season. A commercial atmosphere floats around works of this class, redolent of the manufactory and the shop.[5]

And yet, at the same time, if subsequent versions were to be produced, authors had a chance to do revisions, especially with the invention of moveable type. One book might be reissued with a new introduction. Even within the same edition, "early editions of Byron and Scott, which were usually produced against the clock, contain many corrections, new errors, and some substantial variations," St Clair writes.

Thanks to the invention of moveable type, a book could be altered, transformed, revised, or expanded with each new printing, making it a conversation with reviewers and readers and a revelation of the author's process. It also takes some of the authority away from the author; by making revisions or corrections or responses, it implies they're not infallible.

This changed, however, with the invention of stereotype plates in 1810. These metal plates were made after the text had been set up in moveable type, and while there was an initial cost to create them, they could be put in storage and brought out to create substantially cheaper editions of popular books. It also meant greater print runs were possible, which meant more money. "By 1839 it was said that 100,000 impressions could be taken from one set of plates," St Clair writes. It also brought an end to the practice of making revisions to different editions.

Size matters

When it comes to books, size does matter. Smaller is cheaper, of course. The smaller (and cheaper) book size, the duodecimo, greatly increased in popularity from the first days of the printing press to the mid-eighteenth century when most novels were published in this format. One scholar writes, "it is tempting to view the duodecimo as the early modern equivalent of the twentieth century 'pulp' paperback commonly associated with light fiction for women."[6] We might presume the reference is also comparable to a modern-day, mass-market romance novel.

Not only is smaller cheaper, but it is also more mobile, which is important when it came to the lending libraries or railway station stores—or the pockets of a woman's dress. Many novels were expensive and many of "the new books of the romantic period were too big and too valuable to be taken outside."[7] But with small, cheaply produced books, it became possible to start taking them off the shelf and out of the study. This is important to the development of lending libraries, which made books more affordable for many people. When it came to selling these books at retailers other than traditional bookstores, such as at railway stations, what a reader was looking for in a book changed subtly; from a fancy, expensive volume that would be a prize collectible to a volume that was lightweight and lasted only for the duration of the journey, and could be left behind. Trashy. Throwaway. Books.

The mass-market paperback

The trend of small, cheap, mass-produced books continued into the 1900s with the invention and popularization of the mass-market paperback. A combination of technological innovations, new sales and marketing strategies, and new methods of distribution influenced the editorial content publishers sought—it moved away from what distinguished literary gentlemen could sell to a small, discerning audience to what publishers could predictably sell to a large, predetermined audience. It was another step in the transition from a patronage-based publishing system, in which a wealthy individual funded the publication of a particular work, to a more commercial system that answered to the book-buying public.

Early in the game were the Beadle Brothers, who specialized in publishing Westerns in America in the mid 1800s. Radway writes that they "reasoned that once they had loosely identified an actual audience by inducing it to buy a specific kind of book, it would not be difficult to keep that audience permanently constituted and available for further sales by supplying it with endless imitations of the first success."[8] They were right. And to do this successfully, it required a standardization of both the physical product and the content within.

Later, in the early 1900s, Robert de Graff changed the game with the popularization of the paperback. He took advantage of new technologies in printing, binding, and glue to do massive print runs at a low cost. To distribute all these copies, he turned to the American News Company, which distributed newspapers and magazines to a network of thousands of retailers, such as drugstores, candy shops, and food outlets. To convince these retailers to take a chance on his new product, de Graff instituted a returns policy that plagues publishing to this day (any unsold copies could be returned, at a cost, to the publisher).

Books became cheaper and more accessible than ever. As they became more successful and profitable, it cemented the strategy of creating and selling books as commodities. But not without some downsides.

"When paperbacks first came into publishing, they were seen as lesser than," says Esi Sogah, the romance editor. "All the things that continued to be pubbed in paperback took on that reputation of a pulpy disposable book."

Formula fiction

Romance novels are formulaic. This is not a new critique of
the genre; in an article on "sensation novels" in 1863, the
author wrote of women's fiction: "We watch them advancing
through the intricacies of the plot, as we trace the course of an
x or y through the combinations of an algebraic equation, and
with about as much consciousness of individuality in the
ciphers..." Snark!

Other things that are formulaic: physics, algebra, haikus,
sonnets, recipes, *other* genre fiction. Yet none of these are
judged poorly for adhering to a repeatable form. Romance, on
the other hand, is somehow different. "You don't hear it
leveled against any other genre," agrees Sogah.

Romance novels are not the only literary genre that
adheres to certain plot conventions. "In any genre there are
rules. Mysteries are a great example of this," says Jenn
Northington, former event manager at the independent bookstore WORD in Brooklyn. "There are all these different
subgenres in mystery as well. Each of them has its own set of
conventions." And she points out, "They're not necessarily
bad."

As with other aspects of the romance genre, what
contributes to its success is part of what damns it. In romance,
first we have the meet cute, then the obstacles, then the black
moment when all seems lost, and finally the happy ending.
The formula provides an advantage when it comes to perpetuating the genre. For one thing, it makes it easier to teach the
genre to a new generation of writers by giving them a solid
framework in which to demonstrate their creativity.

But while it helps authors get started, it doesn't necessarily stifle their creativity. Many authors would probably
agree with Esi Sogah when she says, "It's harder to write

within constraints and to be interesting and creative and to hold attention than it is to just do whatever. And I think sometimes people don't see that."

So what is the formula? Is there a rule that the couple must meet by chapter three, have their first kiss on page 69, and confront a nasty villain exactly three-quarters into the story? It's much more vague. Pamela Regis outlines eight elements of the romance novel that are identifiable in most—from the attraction of the two main characters to the "black moment" and the betrothal. But it's even more basic than that: "A romance should have a romance," says Sogah. It should also have a happy ending. Most would argue that it's not a romance without these two elements. And most romance readers would be supremely pissed if their expectations were not met.

The true power in the formula is not just how it standardizes the genre conventions and makes it more easily replicable. The formula is powerful because of how it affects the reading experience, how it makes the reader *feel*, and how that in turn affects sales.

Romance readers know that their romance absolutely will end happily, with the obstacles overcome, the couple in love, a bright future ahead of them, and all subplots and mysteries resolved. Because of this, the element of surprise is "ruined," the stories are labeled "predictable," and it is a horrible, horrible thing everyone should be ashamed of.

Unless, of course, Shakespeare does it. In fact, in some performances of his plays, someone comes out and announces what is about to happen in the next act. This is not to ruin the surprise but to change the reader's focus.

When you know *what* is going to happen, you relax into the story and pay more attention to *how* it happens. When you know that it's "safe" to care for the characters and identify with their feelings because no tragedy will befall them, the reading experience becomes more intense, more personal, more *real*. Recent neurological studies on the effects of reading in the brain show that we experience fiction more deeply than previously thought; it's not just the "language" areas of the brain that light up, but sensory areas as well. When you read the word "cinnamon," your brain is processing it not just as a word but also as a scent.

The formula and certainty of the happy ending allows the reader to focus more intensely on the journey the characters undertake and the transformation they undergo. They can feel it along with the characters. My hunch is that this enhances how our brains already process fiction. The overall effect is one that is more personal and profound that just reading through a collection of scenes that conclude with a moral judgment on how the characters behaved.

Because the reader has been feeling deeply as she reads, the emotional payoff with the happy ending is a tremendous experience. Romance readers know that warm fuzzy feeling, the sigh of delight, and the happily-ever-after glow that comes when finishing a romance. It's not unlike the high of a drug. And it's a high that readers crave again and again.

Readers also bought

For many people, Harlequin is synonymous with romance novel. The Canadian publisher got its start by reprinting English Mills & Boon novels for the North American market. But it was how they marketed those books that led to their tremendous success. Harlequin was "the first in the world to treat books like brand name commodities. Aggressive American-trained, marketing-driven male executives further refined these revolutionary ideas and virtually reinvented book publishing domestically and throughout the world by peddling romance novels like boxes of soap flakes in the very places where women shop,"[9] Paul Grescoe writes in his book *Merchants of Venus: Inside Harlequin and the Empire of Romance.* Indeed, these executives came from companies that did in fact sell boxes of soap.

While Harlequin may have perfected this practice, they did not invent it. The commoditization of literature had been evolving for quite some time. Eighteenth and nineteenth century publishers understood that their success depended on answering the market's demands. And if you were going to give readers the books they wanted, you had to provide them where the readers were looking for books.

Circulating libraries, such as Mudie's, began to spring up in the eighteenth century and became tremendously popular, powerful, and influential by the 1840s. The cost of membership and book borrowing, while pricey, made book reading an option for more people. Being a business, Mudie's sought out ways to increase their profits. One key strategy was the three-volume novel, which enabled one novel to be checked out by multiple readers at the same time, though in different stages of the book. Mudie's also routinely purchased large quantities of novels—if not entire print runs—thus ensuring that a publisher could recoup expenses and make a profit. Naturally, publishers promptly published more novels to Mudie's specifications.

St Clair writes that "the effect of Mudie's declaring, in practice if not explicitly, that a 'good' book was published in three volumes and composed with women and young girls in mind"[10] was that publishers and authors would predominantly create exactly that. The fact that many novels didn't even have an author's name—as many as a third of all novels were just credited to "a lady"—was partially due to concerns for a woman's reputation, especially if she was a woman of quality who ought to be ashamed of writing for money, but it also further reinforced the notion that all the books were interchangeable. They looked the same, the stories were similar, and they were written by the same anonymous author.

This system of course depended on supply and demand: As a certain type of book became more profitable to produce, publishers needed to find manuscripts to print. Implicit in this was the idea that because their motivation was profit and not, say, publishing the finest example of literature ever produced, publishers might select any manuscript that fit their need, regardless of how well written or plotted.

With standardized story elements, a standardized physical product, and a mass audience, selling one book on the reputation of another or on the expectations of the reader became a viable marketing strategy. In the eighteenth and nineteenth centuries, advertising was one of the major costs of producing a book,[11] and this like = like marketing method (especially once Mudie's came along) meant fewer dollars needed to be spent on puffing reviews or newspaper adverts. Instead of guessing what a reader or customer wanted each time, authors and publishers could mitigate their risk and protect their time by generating more of the same.

St Clair explains, "We see the producers trying to commodify the text textually as well as materially by implying that they were broadly similar, within quite narrow limits, both in subject matter and the ideologies they advocated."[12] Janice Radway notes that this continued in the American publishing industry in the nineteenth and twentieth centuries, where it was more cost effective to design an advertising campaign around a type of book rather than an individual title. A television ad from 1980 focuses on Harlequins, generally, instead of a specific title. The camera quickly pans over a big batch of new releases.

Once authors and publishers had become financially dependent on an audience of buyers, they had to satisfy those readers by giving them more of the same. Radway writes, "This new idea of the book as a salable commodity gradually began to alter the organization of the editorial process and eventually the conception of publishing itself."[13] Instead of looking for a unique book that might serve a small, select, and disparate audience, they were keen to satisfy the hunger of a large audience that wanted more books like the ones they'd already read.

To help readers find more of the same, the books were made to look the same. Romances tend to have similar-looking covers (the classic clinch! The dreamy real estate drawings! The cuff links in dark shadows!), similar sounding titles, and, let's face it, similar plots. This was true for early Harlequins, too: "So similar were the fat volumes in appearance (not to mention subject matter) that the more resolute readers would even put their own mark on the backs of the books to indicate whether they had already read them."[14] In the effort to snare readers on a massive scale, the books end up looking and seeming really damn familiar—because they are.

Nowhere is this strategy of like = like more apparent than Amazon's readers also-bought algorithm, which significantly simplifies the decision of what to read next by suggesting titles that similar readers bought, that are similar to the books you've previously purchased, or that are by the same author.

It is an extension of the system that has been developing for centuries. It is a system that is based on marketing books based on their similarities rather than on how they are unique.

This helps to make a commodity out of literature by empha-
sizing what is easily replicable more than what is special.

However, each romance novel is special in some way.
Agents and publishers are always on the lookout for "fresh"
new stories and voices and authors strive to deliver this. As
readers, we want a book to surprise and delight us—while
still delivering the love story and happy ending we expect.
And we know to find those stories by looking out for certain
visual clues, whether the book is "By a Lady" or has Fabio on
the cover.

In this volume-based business, everything is geared
toward making the product easily replicable, whether it's
through the "formulaic" plot; the standard length, size, and
format; the technological innovations in printing that allow
for massive quantities to be cheaply produced; or marketing
based on how one book is similar to a hundred others. These
strategies have made romance a huge success, but they have
also contributed to its bad reputation.

One commenter to a *USA Today* article about romance
novels writes, "I can tell you exactly why it doesn't garner
respect: Because it is a book factory and they can churn them
out like the cheap dime novels of old."[15] From the beginning,
what made the popular romance novel a commercial success
prohibited it from being a critical success. It never had a
chance of becoming respectable fiction.

A tale of two readerships

And then there's William Wordsworth. He's the quintessential
nineteenth century romantic poet and author of such classics
as *I Wandered Lonely as a Cloud* and *The Leech-Gatherer.*
Though he is required reading in many high school and
college courses, he was not widely read in his time. His story

highlights some of the tensions surrounding who and what literature is for.

In a time when the Industrial Revolution was in full swing, with its crowded cities and stinking factories, the Romantic Movement glorified nature and the simple agrarian life. But for all that Wordsworth lauded the rural poor, his books weren't exactly accessible to them. "Wordsworth may have believed that the rural poor were more sensitive to literature than gentlemen, but he did not number many leech gatherers among his readers,"[16] St Clair writes. His collection, *The Excursion,* was produced in quarto size, and for the price of one copy, a reader in Salisbury could have purchased 100 pigs.[17] However, his books weren't the only pricey ones.

His print runs were small—around 500 copies compared to Jane Austen's books (2,000) or Sir Walter Scott's Waverley novels (tens of thousands). He barely sold any copies in his lifetime, yet today, he's part of the canon.

If certain books were expensive to produce and had little hope of selling, generating a profit, or being widely read, why create them at all?

Mary Poovey, a professor at New York University, gets to the heart of the matter: "The Romantic definition of literary value made it difficult for authors of genres that were popular —whose value as commodities was unmistakable—to claim that their works were also valuable in aesthetic terms."[18] Likewise, if Wordsworth and others like him couldn't justify the production of his work in commercial terms, he had to find another way. The answer was to elevate one form of literature as intellectually superior and denigrate the other type as trash.

The effects of this split between the lofty literary reader and the rest of the poor shmucks who read rubbish was profound, as Mary Poovey points out:

The eighteenth-century publishing industry helped create two nations of readers...one, a tiny minority, practiced discriminating fact from fiction by reading expensive, time-consuming books that commented self-consciously on their own epistemological and stylistic status; and the other, the vast majority, sought escape and self-improvement by reading cheap works that were rapidly consumed."[19]

In 1858, Wilkie Collins writes of his discovery of one of these readerships, the "unknown reading public" of millions who read cheap literature "for its amusement more than for its information." He points out that "None of the gentlemen who are so good as to guide my taste in literary matters had ever directed my attention to these mysterious publications."

Here we start to see the split between Serious Readers and people who devoured cheap books as if they were potato chips—deliciously but thoughtlessly, and to the detriment of their health. A distinction is made between books that are hard and books that are easily consumed. "Easy" books are also assumed to be read quickly and, as Sogah says, "people that don't read like that don't think you can have any meaningful interaction" with the book.

When modern day romance readers and advocates champion the romance genre based on its financial success, we reinforce this long-held split between two types of readers and two types of books. It's especially clear when romance readers defend the genre by first pointing out that romance is a billion dollar industry (says someone who has repeated that herself more than a few times) or that many bestseller slots are occupied by lady romance authors.

I have even noticed romance fans defending *Fifty Shades of Grey* because of its sales, but quickly distancing themselves from the quality of the writing. Talking about romance as "trashy" and "commercial" reinforces the idea that the primary value of these books is the sales they generate, and not the ideals they champion, how the stories fit into larger cultural conversations, the thoughts the books provoke, or even the quality of writing.

Overall, it seems the reputation of romance will be inextricably linked with the way our culture values popular, affordable, "low-brow" entertainment and the people who enjoy it.

THE ROMANCE NOVEL INDUSTRY

ROMANCE
is
a billion dollar
industry

Estimated annual
total sales value
of romance in

2013

$1.08 billion

9,513
Romance
ISBNs in
2013

Romance novels are 17% of the adult
fiction category.

It outsells almost all other fiction.

Popular fiction genres

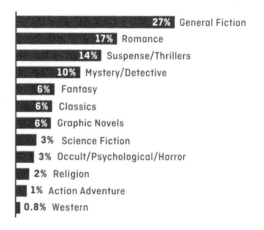

- 27% General Fiction
- 17% Romance
- 14% Suspense/Thrillers
- 10% Mystery/Detective
- 6% Fantasy
- 6% Classics
- 6% Graphic Novels
- 3% Science Fiction
- 3% Occult/Psychological/Horror
- 2% Religion
- 1% Action Adventure
- 0.8% Western

WHO
is the romance
reader?

MALE 16%

84% FEMALE

Popular formats for romance

- 39% E-books
- 32% Mass-market paperback
- 18% Trade paperback
- 9% Hardcover
- 1% Audio
- 1% Other

Romance readers primarily find out about new books from FRIENDS & FAMILY

THE STORY
is the #1
reason factor
in a reader's
purchasing decision

Popular romance subgenres

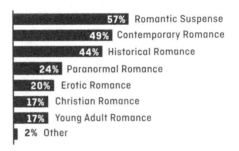

57% Romantic Suspense
49% Contemporary Romance
44% Historical Romance
24% Paranormal Romance
20% Erotic Romance
17% Christian Romance
17% Young Adult Romance
2% Other

63% think there is not enough diversity in characters and settings*

47% say they don't care what's on the cover*

Sources: The Nielson Group Book Industry Year In Review 2013, Nielsen Books & Consumer Tracker, BISAC Romance, BISAC Romance, Romance Writers of America, *The Dangerous Books For Girls study

FIVE

HOW LADY AUTHORS DRIVE
INNOVATION IN PUBLISHING

WOMEN GOT into the business of writing novels early. There was an increase in female literacy in the eighteenth and nineteenth centuries, creating a market of readers for the Lady Author. Mass-produced items were becoming available, thanks to the Industrial Revolution, which meant that women had more leisure time when she could just buy candles instead of make her own. She could also write while still maintaining her traditional role of daughter, wife, mother, and housekeeper.

The Lady Author continued to be on the frontline of innovation in publishing, whether in the shift to mass-market paperback or the digital revolution. "There was a sense that the romance consumer and romance writer were at the forefront of what was happening in publishing," says Esi Sogah, the romance editor at Kensington. "And therefore a good place to try new things and be innovative because if anyone was going to respond to it, this is where you would get it. And then you could roll it out to other areas."

Indeed, publishers such as Avon do this. "We definitely start everything," says senior Avon editor Tessa Woodward, who is credited with helping Avon to launch the trendy and popular New Adult subgenre and Avon's digital-first line. "Any test they want to run they start it with the romance writers because romance writers are savvier, and more willing to experiment. It's definitely not because they are women, it just happens that a lot of the innovation comes out of the romance world."

Qualities of the romance writing community allow it to try new things, grow its readership, and support its authors, which in turn promote the overall success of the genre and industry. The fine line between reader and writer, the high volume of production that allows for risk taking, and the lack of prestige to lose when it comes to trying new things have all contributed to the success of the romance industry. It's why romance authors are able to go from Jane Austen and other Lady Authors scribbling away in their drawing rooms to a billion-dollar industry today.

A close connection between authors and readers

"Women...are the chief readers of novels; they are also, of late at least, the chief writers of them" William Rathbone Greg wrote in the nineteenth century.[1] Even today, so many romance authors were readers of the genre first. This means that they are well positioned to know their market and to instinctively know which holes exist—what is the story they want to read but can't find, for example? So many authors, myself included, have a moment similar to one bestselling Regency Romance author Julia Quinn describes on her website:

That's when she looked at the book next to the tub of now-empty Ben & Jerry's. It was a romance. "I could write one of those," she thought.

And so she did.

Today, when those romance readers get the idea of "hey, I could write one!" they'll find innumerable resources to help them navigate everything from completing the manuscript to getting it published and then promoting it. Romance Writers of America (RWA), the trade organization founded in 1980, provides extensive resources for writers on everything from crafting their manuscript, getting it published to promoting one's work. Whether it's how to write a steamy sex scene or what clauses to watch out for in a contract, RWA and its members are there to offer advice.

"Are you going to nationals?" is a question probably only understood by the most devoted of the romance community. It refers to the national conference held by RWA each summer, where bestselling and aspiring authors mingle, trade secrets are presented in workshops, and hundreds of authors gather for a book signing to promote literacy. The Rita awards, "The Oscars of romance publishing," are handed out in a formal ceremony. I have also noted that there is a particularly loud, high-pitched sound to this conference, when thousands of women gather to revel in their shared love of romance novels.

While RWA is a national organization, its members are connected through local chapters, social media, and online classes and informed by a monthly print publication. Through the extensive resources they provide and the connections facilitated between authors, agents, and editors, RWA helps the genre get ahead by helping individual authors succeed in their dream of romance publication. According to my friends in the literary world, nothing like this exists for them.

But what really makes RWA so successful—indeed the whole romance industry—is a pay-it-forward mentality among the community. To be sure, there is jealousy, fierce competition, and the like, but on the whole, the women in this group help each other out. "We're very collaborative. There's a lot of sharing," says bestselling author and indie publishing powerhouse Bella Andre.

It is not unheard of for a bestselling author to critique a new writer's manuscript. In fact, I learned more about the writing of romance from one session with a bestselling author, in which she ripped my sample chapters to shreds, scolded me for head hopping, and pointed out where I had achieved the "Regency voice." Even agents and editors who rejected my work took a moment to point out why and how I could improve.

On email loops dedicated to particular areas of interest, whether a subgenre (historical, erotica) or type of publishing (independent or aligned with a particular publisher), knowledge is widely and freely shared (sometimes too much—my inbox is constantly plagued by the digest versions of the three loops I subscribe to). Whether technical questions, recommendations for cover artists and copy editors, or general best practices, romance authors do not keep information to themselves.

One perfect example is the inclusion of purchase links at the end of an e-book, when a reader is most likely to buy the author's next work. This is a practice a few self-published authors pioneered and recommended to others when they found it successful. Traditional publishing is now following their lead.

It is also not unusual for authors to recommend another writer's book to their fans. This is probably due to the fact that most fans read A LOT of books, so recommending your friend's latest novel doesn't mean a reader won't buy your new one. She'll probably pick up both. There is room for everyone to succeed. Also, the tone of conversation between authors and readers is more like that of friend to friend rather than brand to consumer, so of course you would tell your friends about the last awesome book you read.

And then there is social media, which romance authors have taken to like ducks to water. Many have thousands or tens of thousands or even hundreds of thousands of followers. But it's not the numbers that matter: It's the conversation between readers and authors as *humans*. "My readers are more than just readers, they are a family," said author Brenda Jackson at a conference on popular romance in Washington, DC. As they write, authors can solicit feedback from their fans or request help in naming the hero's ancestral estate or the heroine's dog. I have even enlisted the help of my Facebook fans in determining the title of one of my books. Rather than writing alone in a garret, the romance author is constantly connecting with her audience.

The romance writer, then, is uniquely positioned to understand what her reader wants and needs from a story because she is talking to her readers on a daily basis in an intimate, human way.

High volume = low cost = less risk

Romance is a volume business and authors and publishers make it work by publishing a lot of books, particularly a lot of connected books.

Romance novels are often part of a series, which means that while an individual novel will focus on one couple's love story, all the books in a particular series will be set in the same fictional world with recurring characters, many of whom will get their chance to star in a novel of their own. For readers, picking up a book in a familiar series is like going to a party where you already know the other guests—it's a lot less stressful and more relaxing when you know what to wear, who is going to be there, and what everyone will be talking about.

For authors and publishers, it's a way to sell a book without selling a book. If you fell in love with the hero's scene-stealing brother in the first novel, it'll be easy to sell you the next one in which he is now the hero. An excerpt or blurb of an upcoming work in the back of the book—and now "buy" links—entice the reader and make it easy for them to purchase. The author, then, just sold two books (or more!) and only needed to market one.

When a reader is hooked on a series, there is more leeway with the pricing. While someone might waffle over spending $2.99 to try a new author, if she is obsessed and committed to a series, she will not think twice about clicking "download now" on the sixth one in the series, even though it's $7.99. I have been that reader, so hooked on a series that nothing— not a high price or late hour—will keep me from the next book.

Less time spent marketing means more free time to write books. It's not unusual for a romance author to write two a year—maybe even more. Because most writers write many books a year, it's less risky for them to try something new. This might manifest as writing under a new name in a different subgenre, which allows them to appeal to different audiences and put out more books per year without saturating one part of the market.

An author might also try a different type of hero or heroine or a twist on the traditional plot formula, or write a novel exploring darker themes instead of the usual romp. On a large scale, these experiments can push the boundaries of the genre and start new trends. On a personal scale, it can keep a writer from getting bored.

The rise of self-publishing and the low cost of producing a work mean that an individual can be even more experimental in the stories she publishes and the way she markets them. Before the prevalence of self-publishing, an author had to convince the gatekeepers in New York City (who then have to convince the buyers at the sales accounts); now she just has to believe in her work and put it out there, armed with advice and best practices from her fellow authors. Self-published authors, especially, will look at their sales numbers to determine if they should start a new series or keep going with what's working, allowing them to take more informed risks.

If it fails? C'est la vie. It might have been a few months' work, but there are more books waiting to be written and due soon. The quick time to market is another plus for the genre fiction writer.

The typewriter paradox

"Historically the phrase—woman's profession—would be a big wet blanket to any respectable trade," Hanna Rosin writes in *The End of Men: And the Rise of Women*, a book about the newly changing dynamics between the sexes. "Wages would drop, men would flee, and all the prestige would drain out of the job," A Columbia University historian Alice Kessler-Harris has called it the typewriter paradox: "Women master a machine or a set of skills that opens up new job opportunities for them, and then that job becomes immediately devalued."[2]

In the eighteenth and nineteenth centuries, women were "allowed" to write novels because they were low-brow literature and mindless entertainment for the young and idle, and men hadn't deemed it their important and valuable domain. Novel writing was low-paying hackwork even then, dependent on churning out one book after another. While it was respectable work for a woman (relative to other professions), it was hardly an envious position.

While the novel as an art form has gained critical respectability, women's fiction hasn't done so nearly as much. But part of it is because women read it and write it. When asked why romance had a bad reputation, 69 percent of survey respondents said, "Because women write it and read it." While there are excellent, critically acclaimed novels written by women, the literary canon is still dominated by men. Culturally, we still devalue things deemed "women's work," whether they are jobs like teacher, secretary, nurse, homemaker, or romance novelist.

The positive aspect, however, is that, at least with the romance genre, this low visibility has allowed its constituents a certain freedom to experiment, to innovate, or to seize whatever opportunity is presented because no one is watching over the collective shoulder. With little prestige to lose, the Lady Author is free to explore and capitalize on new opportunities, especially independent publishing.

Romance writers were among the first to try self-publishing and to date they have been the ones to find the most success at it. Indie publishing advocate Hugh Howey shows data revealing that romance authors were earning more from e-books than those in literary fiction or other genres.[3] "A lot of the self pub came out of the romance world, or a lot of it is, by any other name, romance," says Tessa Woodward, the Avon editor.

While e-books have transformed the publishing industry dramatically, independently published e-books have been considered to be of poor quality because they are so cheap— 99 cents, or even free. They are also presumed to be inferior because they haven't been produced by a traditional New York City publisher. The CEO of Zebra Publishing, Steven

Zacharius, inflamed the self-publishing community by voicing his concern that readers "might not even know if they're buying a book that was professionally edited versus one that was self-published."[4] In fact, the self-published authors that are the most successful are also the ones that are the most professional in the production of their books; many enlist a copy editor and a content editor. Others even stage their own photo shoots for the cover art. But that is hardly the popular perception.

There was no prestige in independent publishing or "vanity" publishing, but romance authors have had little prestige to lose, anyway, so they were among the first to head out into this Wild West and the first to strike gold.

There were a few reasons for their success. "Romance authors have had a singular chance in that our readers were online first and that allowed us to innovate," says indie publishing phenomenon and advocate Courtney Milan, whose historical romances include some of the smartest and most beloved heroines.

The popular image of someone tech savvy may be a dude, but that's not accurate. "It turns out women are our new lead adopters," *The Atlantic* reports on findings by Intel researcher Genevieve Bell. "When you look at Internet usage, it turns out women in Western countries use the Internet 17 percent more every month than their male counterparts...the majority of technology users are women in their 40s, 50s, and 60s."[5]

Those readers went online because traditional publishers weren't meeting their needs. "I think a lot of people think romance readers are looking for any old book and it's interchangeable and we're not," Milan says. "So they started cutting down and in response romance readers asked 'how can I get these books?' and Amazon and buying them online was the first answer. I think romance readers were some of

the first to flee to digital." Decreasing shelf space in bookstores meant readers couldn't find what they were looking
for. If a store didn't have the first four books in a romance
series, the typical reader wasn't going to start at book five.
Similarly, many readers discover an author they like and then
proceed to work their way through her often extensive back-
list, which most bookstores no longer have the shelf space
for. She would go elsewhere to find the exact books she
wished to read, and that elsewhere was online.

A romance reader is a voracious reader, and digital made
it cheaper, easier, and faster to get the books she wanted—
without *another* embarrassing trip to the store. Those cringe-
inducing covers, too, weren't such a problem anymore when
no one could see them and make disparaging remarks. The e-
reader has served a lot of needs for the romance reader.

Independent publishing also made it possible for a whole
new variety of books to find an audience. Because traditional
publishers have to convince a buyer at a mass merchandise
account, whose main consideration is what will sell without
offending anyone, it's a bigger risk for them to try an author,
genre or subject matter that isn't tried and true. Therefore
some books couldn't find a market.

"There were also books that weren't being published by
regular print publishers," Milan says. One example of this is
erotica, which would be a hard sell to traditional distributors
like Walmart. "Ellora's Cave and Samhain came along and
started getting into the e-book thing even before Amazon
came up with the Kindle. That meant there were a handful of
early adopters in romance."

Because romance readers weren't having their needs met
in traditional markets, they gravitated toward new ones. And
romance authors, with their close connection to their readership, were able to join them there. Stigmas about the

respectability of indie publishing weren't much of a consideration—romance didn't have much respectability anyway. A financial model in which they publish many books instead of laboring over one for years meant that it could make financial sense to publish quickly, cheaply, and often on their own and forgo an advance from a traditional publisher. The conditions were just right for them to capitalize on this new opportunity.

SIX

FOR LOVE AND MONEY

WOMEN WRITING FOR MONEY ABOUT WOMEN MARRYING FOR LOVE

THERE WAS an audible gasp in the ballroom at a New Jersey romance conference when a bestselling author stood up to address the crowd and confessed, "My name is Eloisa James and I write for money."

Writers aren't supposed to be motivated by something as basic as money, and they're certainly not supposed to talk about it if they are. We are supposed to be starving artists, nobly scratching out manuscripts in cold attics while subsisting on bread and water (or more likely, coffee, wine, and chocolate) just for the love of it. But the long history of Lady Authors shows that many were motivated to write for financial reasons, and not only to have some extra pin money for a cute hat, but simply to survive. This mix of women and money had an effect on how the genre was perceived.

Writing for money

"Many are offended when writers talk about money," author Shannon Hale writes in a blog post entitled *The nitty gritty on authors, signings, and filthy lucre*[1]. "Art and commerce shouldn't mix! Authors are artists and shouldn't make decisions based on dirty filthy lucre!" When there is a discussion taking into account a book's salability before writing it, or about whether to mail a free copy to a fan, or if an author should quit the day job, it's a reminder that authors live in the world and need to eat; as such, they are just as likely to answer to the market as to some divine inspiration. This practicality can be a startling contrast when one writes aspirational fiction, often about heroines who are heiresses themselves or catch rich husbands; in other words, women who don't have to worry about money. For a Lady Author to talk of money is, for a moment, to pull the veil back on the fantasy.

When women write for money, it's particularly troubling. As I've mentioned before, writing was one of the only semi-respectable professions for women that they could do from home; this marked some of their first steps into the marketplace. Giving women money also changed the dynamics in personal relationships and altered who had the power to make decisions and call the shots in the household. In an era such as the eighteenth and nineteenth centuries, in which the household is supposed to be the microcosm for the entire culture at large, a wife making money can be philosophically troubling or annoying if you're a man who wants to spend the money on gin instead of food.

In order to feel better about women writing for money, "we were glad to think that the money went to relieve the necessitous, and we pictured to ourselves lonely women struggling for a maintenance," George Eliot writes in her essay *Silly Novels by Lady Novelists*, "or wives and daughters devoting themselves to the production of 'copy' out of pure heroism, perhaps to pay their husband's debts, or to purchase luxuries for a sick father."[2] Indeed, many wrote out of a desperate need.

The other truth not often talked about is that the money a woman earns from writing romance fiction is often not enough.

In his book *Women Writing about Money: Women's Fiction in England 1790–1820*, Edward Copeland does the math on how much popular nineteenth century lady novelists made over the course of their lifetimes. It's not great:

The highly touted successes of Burney and More, or Maria Edgeworth and Susan Ferrier...must be put in terms of lifetime earnings to become significant...Charlotte Smith's earnings over a 19-year period of constant production and desperate labor come to only £4,500 or £5,000 total, most of it consumed as soon as it was received. Jane Austen's records of profit in her publishing history read as a series of unfortunate misjudgments of the business.[3]

Even today, for every E. L. James, Nora Roberts, Sylvia Day, or self-published author pulling in six figures a month, there are thousands more who won't turn a profit on their writing, or at least not for a long while. In the documentary on the romance genre, *Love Between the Covers*,[4] more than a few authors mention stories of selling their first book and getting a small advance, only to have their husband say it's not enough and they still need to have dinner on the table on time. Writing brought in much needed money, but it was often insufficient. Nevertheless, it was something.

While Eliot actually claims that many Lady Authors didn't write out of need at all (though it was true in many cases), she notes that this perception that they did had an interesting effect on the critical reception of the lady novel:

"Under these impressions we shrank from criticizing a lady's novel: Her English might be faulty, but, we said to ourselves, her motives are irreproachable; her imagination may be uninventive, but her patience is untiring." By not wanting to diminish the efforts of noble women making an attempt at an honorable living, they weren't held to a higher standard—the standard, presumably, of well-educated men's writing—and the entire genre of women's fiction was done a disservice. Without being challenged, authors were allowed to get by doing well enough. By not having experts determine what is well executed and what is rubbish—after actually reading it —these women presumably had no idea how to improve their writing. While the genre of romance has not received much review attention then or now, I don't think this is the only reason.

While the prospect of women writing may have been troubling to society and while it may not have brought it enough money all of the time, it still set a precedent of women earning money from their own brains instead of their bodies and having some measure of freedom and independence or authority in their household.

"Look back at what Jane Austen started," Eloisa James says. "What she did with *Pride and Prejudice* was start something that allowed hundreds of thousands of women after her to make a living, to run families, to make more than their husbands, to not have a husband. She provided a road for all these women to become entrepreneurs in their own right."

Women marrying for love

One of the first things that we learn about Mr. Darcy, the quintessential romance hero, is that he has an income of "ten thousand a year." At which point, Mrs. Bennett's eyes nearly bug out of her head because, oh my lord, if one of her girls could land him, then all their problems would be solved and their futures would be certain. Money = security. For a long time the only way for women to gain security was through an advantageous marriage.

Women's fiction was a way to negotiate these tensions and anxieties between two sometimes conflicting expectations: that a woman should marry for love and that she must also marry someone who could support her financially.

In *Pride and Prejudice* (1813), Elizabeth Bennett famously refuses Darcy's first proposal because it is delivered without respect and received without love. Austen writes, "In spite of her deeply rooted dislike, she could not be insensible to the compliment of such a man's affection."[5] The significance of her refusal of such an eligible and wealthy bachelor is heightened because the Bennett women are facing a future of poverty if Mr. Bennett dies before one of them weds well.

Though the proposal may appeal to the head (or purse), it is repulsive to the heart and shockingly, that alone can be considered reason enough to refuse (though not to Mrs. Bennett). Elizabeth is not oblivious to her family's situation, either. Here we see the tension not only between love and money, but also between the individual and the group. In refusing Darcy, Elizabeth is prioritizing her own happiness over the comforts and security of her family. Love has a high price.

However, Darcy finds love a compelling reason to overlook other practical considerations in the selection of a spouse. "His sense of her inferiority, of its being a degradation, of the family obstacles..."[6] all pale in significance to a love he tried to, but could not, suppress. In the end, when

Darcy proposes a second time, the reader and Elizabeth know it is based on love and admiration, not merely a reluctant physical attraction, or because she needed the money. She can accept with her head and heart. Lucky for her, she doesn't have to choose between the heart and the pocketbook. That is the fantasy.

Not every heroine had to sit around, minding her manners, waiting for a suitable proposal. Many novels of the time featured heroines who worked. In his book on women writers and money, Copeland looks extensively at how these authors wrote about heroines and employment during this time period. The message changed depending on the type of work or the publisher—and the intended audience. "In a pointed distinction to a writer like Austen, Minerva [Press] writers refuse to rescue their heroines from the experience of employment. They give their heroine the usual prerequisites at the conclusion, of course, a husband with utopian virtues and large estates, but not until *after* the heroine has tested the waters of employment and triumphed."

There are a variety of paths for heroines take on the way to her happy-ever-after. A novel is a powerful way for a woman to get a glimpse of alternate realities—work, not working, what it feels like to refuse a man with ten thousand a year. I know my reaction to that refusal changed with subsequent readings—as I became more financially secure myself, I thought Lizzie was less mad.

Even today, when heroines and real life women can and do support themselves, we still see a diversity of heroine experiences—some conveniently fall for and land billionaires and some make their own damn money. Some are heiresses who marry impoverished heroes. The range of experiences offers a telling clue to what is vexing an author about the time the story is written.

While it's not polite to talk about money, romance provides a way for women to think about it, talk about it, and examine how much it matters in their lives. The romance genre has empowered untold numbers of women to earn their own money so they can afford to marry for love.

SEVEN

ROMANCE VERSUS REALISM

YOU DON'T REALLY BELIEVE THAT DO YOU?

ONE OF THE most frequent critiques of romance novels is that they are unrealistic and women are at dire risk of basing their lives on silly ideas they read about in some cheap book. Echoing fears articulated in an 1855 article "What is the Harm of Novel-Reading?"[1] the author details the downward spiral of a novel reader, led astray by her expectations of a gentleman's love and fortune. Not only were her expectations outrageous, but she was also duped by the "gentleman" who "abused her credulity" before abandoning her. Poor, stupid, foolish girl. If only someone had told her that the books were unrealistic!

When I asked non-romance readers to describe a romance novel, a majority of respondents *wrote in* "unrealistic."

People tend to be quite vague about what, exactly, is unrealistic about a romance novel—especially in comparison to a comic book or science-fiction work. But they "just know" that romance novels are fluffy fantasy books that delude women.

Some readers might point out that, at no point in time, was the romance shelved in the nonfiction section. Others might question what is so unrealistic about love? But that is missing the point.

Why have romance novels been singled out as unrealistic?

Why romance is unrealistic but science fiction is not

Of all the literary forms, it is romance novels that are so often decried as unrealistic—not science fiction, fantasy, murder mysteries or comic books, for example. Each of these forms depicts emotions that are recognizable to humans, and they often resolve in an emotionally just way (similarly to the happy ending in romance). But they also defy laws of science, logic and statistical probability (every murder mystery is solved, every battle is won by the good guys). These genres are obviously unrealistic but no one slams them for it precisely because they are obviously so.

Even though romance novels feature human emotions, emotionally just conclusions and as many men in tights as comic books, they are singled out as implausible. This claim is not just reserved for the obviously unrealistic stories featuring vampires, werewolves, shape shifters, and other worlds, but the historicals, the contemporaries, the ones we could fact check.

It seems there is a line of "too real" and romance novels cross it, while still being fantasy and fictional. It's a lot like the Uncanny Valley, a term coined by robotics professor Masahiro Mori:

As the appearance of a robot is made more human, some human observers' emotional response to the robot will become increasingly positive and empathic, until a point is reached beyond which the response quickly becomes that of strong revulsion. However, as the robot's appearance continues to become less distinguishable from that of a human being, the emotional response becomes positive once again and approaches human-to-human empathy levels. This area of repulsive response aroused by a robot with appearance and motion between a "barely human" and "fully human" entity is called the uncanny valley.[2]

In a science fiction novel, comic book or cartoon, the depictions of the actors are so outrageous and obviously fictional that there is almost no way an adult would mistake them for real life. They are the robot that is obviously a robot. But a romance novel, which acrobatically walks a fine line between fantasy and absolutely plausible, realistic but idealized, is like the robot that is *too* human.

"We will accept a synthetic human that looks and moves realistically... but only up to a point; our satisfaction drops precipitately once the resemblance becomes close enough to nearly—but not quite—fool us," Margaret Talbot writes in an article on the Uncanny Valley in the *New Yorker*. The descriptions of most heroes, for example, portray larger than life (cartoonish?) versions of masculinity. They are well over six feet tall, with eight-pack abs, broad shoulders, and legs like tree trunks. Many a heroine, particularly in the old school romances, has a waist so slim the hero's hands span around it. There are a ridiculous number of heroines with violet eyes and hair that never needs to be brushed. They talk like humans, they feel like humans, they act like humans...but they don't look like any humans that mere mortal readers know. Perhaps the fantastic physical descriptions with the all too human emotions just make some people uncomfortable.

In the same article, the author goes on to write about that "which felt emotionally human yet didn't pretend to *be* human."[3] Romance authors and readers prize emotional relatability in their characters. We may not know anyone in our day-to-day lives who looks like these paper people, we may not have traveled to the small towns in Texas or Scottish castles or wherever else these books are set, and we may not have had the same life experiences. What matters is if the emotions ring true.

Why we're afraid women won't know the difference

Hand in hand with the claim that romance novels are unrealistic is the fear that women won't know the difference. A lady reader might feel terrible that she does not have violet eyes, or she might refuse a perfectly good suitor because he is not the extreme paragon of masculinity described in the pages of a romance. A lady might live her real life as if the stuff of fiction was true. She might—gasp—dare to expect an egalitarian relationship where both people are free to be their true selves. Or she might refuse to work, expecting to suddenly inherit a fortune or land a duke. She might be duped by a rogue masquerading as a "gentleman." There can be real life consequences to the reading of fiction.

This is ridiculous—now. Mostly. But in the nineteenth century, this was a very real fear. The novel, and the idea that it should realistically portray the world, was just gaining prominence. Romance was traditionally understood to mean a fantastic, extravagant tale. Indeed, that is the primary definition in the dictionaries today.

While the terms romance and novel have often been held in opposition to each other, over time they have been "confounded together"[4] and merged to become the romance novel as many understand it today. In fact, the traditional definition of the terms romance and novel directly contradict each other.

But that hasn't stopped them from being used interchangeably. Below we can see how the traditional elements from a gothic romance can be easily paralleled in what we might term a courtship novel:

> *For the transmutation of a romance to a novel.*
> *Where you find...*
> *A castle...Put a house*
> *A blood-stain'd dagger...Put a fan*
> *A heroine...Versatile enough not to be changed*
> *Assassins...Put killing glances*
> *A monk...Put an old steward*
> *A witch...Put an old housekeeper*
> *A midnight murder...Put a marriage*

Thus, the trappings and the props are distinct to each narrative type but are easily translated, suggesting more similarities in story arc, plot, and characters (particularly the heroine). However, this table also reinforces the premise that novels are more realistic than romances. Castles do exist, but houses are more prevalent. Housekeepers with witchlike qualities are probably encountered with more frequency than witches. Clara Reeves provides a very succinct definition in *The Progress of Romance*: "The Romance...describes what never happened nor is likely to happen."[5] But the novel is supposed to represent real life as we know it.

Thus, romances could be easily mistaken for novels, especially by the audience of "poor, ignorant girls" and "silly females." Presumably women didn't have enough intellect, reason, or education to distinguish between the two, especially if some elements of the book seemed so very realistic. Or, more like it, these types of novels presented a world that was a tantalizing picture of the one they lived in...but better.

In her book *The True Story of the Novel,* Margaret Anne Doody writes, "The proliferation of conduct books in the eighteenth century bears witness to social fears that females, influenced by the pernicious novel, might get above them- selves, take themselves too seriously."[6] Because the novel looked so similar to real life in terms of portraying humans on earth, obeying the laws of physics and society while also painting a picture of a daring woman succeeding and finding real love in that setting, it wasn't totally implausible that women would believe them to be real or at the very least aspirational. Or inspirational.

Dismissing the books as unrealistic isn't necessarily a slight on how well or how accurately the author wrote her story, but about the "crazy" ideas these novels explored and celebrated. Crazy ideas like freedom for women, mutual respect between men and women, true love, or a woman's worth.

Sweet, sweet fantasy

But the fact remains that romance is fantasy by definition. Readers also *want* it to be fantasy. The vast majority of people read romance for escape and entertainment and to experience lives unlike their own. It's not that they are avoiding real life, but we deal with enough socks on the floor in real life, thanks (I dare you to show me a romance hero who has left his socks on the floor when the hamper is *right there*). This is not a new thing: "What has to be read in the workshop and kitchen must be enacted at club and boudoir," Margaret Oliphant writes in 1858,[7] meaning that we don't wish to see an exact, totally accurate, really real depiction of our lives when reading escapist fiction. We want the better version. We want the idealized version.

Some readers within the genre will point out major discrepancies between romance novels and reality—thus highlighting how romance is an idealized, fantastical world. For example, the sheer number of billionaires and dukes strolling through the pages of romance novels vastly outnumber those in reality. Jackie Horne of the blog Romance Novels for Feminists has done the math and found that in real life, dukes made up only 0.0001735 percent of the population of England in 1818. Narrowing the numbers to just the gentry only, 0.00868 percent were dukes. For perspective, her survey of romance novel titles showed that 1.7 percent have "duke" in the title. I'd argue that the number of romances with this type of hero is even higher.[8] As of this writing, there are 492 billionaires in America[9] and only 11 of them are under the age of 40.[10] Amazon shows 14,938 results for "kindle billionaire romance."

The prevalence of disease-free rakes—charming men who have vast amounts of sexual experience with a large number of women—is another common element of romance requiring a reader's suspension of disbelief. Historical author Courtney Milan has crunched some numbers and writes on her blog that "a rake in Victorian times who had unprotected penetrative sex with 500 women had a 0.000000000000000000001 percent chance of sleeping with nobody who had diseases.... Even if you imagine that our rake in question had some awesome rake superpower that allowed him to skip the worst cases, so that he only slept with women who were 99 percent likely to be clean, a rake who slept with 500 women who were 99 percent likely to have nothing has a 0.6 percent chance of avoiding someone who was infected."[11] We prize those sexually experienced heroes and gloss over the likelihood that they will have picked up a disease or two in the course of their amorous education and possibly passed it along to the heroine. Who wants to read about incurable syphilis in one's escapist literature?

The priority for the romance writer is creating a story that will captivate the reader, whisk her away from her day-to-day life so she can explore important issues. With a rich hero, one doesn't need to worry about how the couple will pay the bills, but can focus on their emotional needs and relationship dynamics. Of course we know that sexual promiscuity increases the likelihood of STIs, which is why we explore sexuality through romance novels—it's safer (and you don't have to shave your legs). A novel that ignores mundane issues like socks on the floor and what's for dinner is free to contemplate bigger and more significant things.

Romance novels aren't any less valid because they portray fantasies. The purpose of some fiction is to depict life as we know it, but romance novels have a different purpose: to show life as it could be.

Uh-oh, high standards

Romance novels give women higher expectations for life, sex, relationships, and partners, usually men. No one paints such a grotesque yet elegant picture of this *and why* than William Giraldi in his blistering piece for *The New Republic*:

At the height of the moronic craze over *Fifty Shades of Grey,* I happened upon a newscast showing a "lifestyle" story in which a camera crew had marauded into the home of a painfully white-bread couple from some nook of New England. According to the missus, their sagging sex life had just been buttressed by her embrace of the Fifty Shades trilogy, and the prevailing mood of this piece, I recall, was one of willing but abject exploitation. As the wife read aloud her favorite lines from one of the books—sentences, as you know, of such galactic ineptitude it was hard to believe a primate could have written them—the husband sat beside her on the sofa, blinking at the camera with a look of the most shell-shocked capitulation. It was unclear whether or not the wife had acquired the battery-operated sex utensils employed in the trilogy, but it couldn't have been clearer that her porcine husband was being put through a nightly, ghastly regimen of sexual aerobics, a regimen for which he was neither physically nor emotionally suited. He was a cardiac catastrophe in waiting, someone who'd been perfectly content to pass his evenings with TV and pizza. But then along came these blasted books and wrecked his American right to glut and sloth.[12]

This poor, poor man. The heart bleeds for this man who must (horrors!) attempt to satisfy his wife sexually. Or talk to her. Or do things for her for which he is neither "physically nor emotionally suited." Or give up nights of eating crap and watching TV and feeling nothing. Of course Christian Grey and other every other romance hero succeed where this man fails. The romance hero is more than willing to satisfy the heroine in all of the ways. If he is not physically or emotionally suited to a lifetime of true love and hot sex, the romance hero will change.

Bestselling author Tessa Dare says "women are constantly told its fantasy to expect fidelity, respect and orgasms in this life and to seek the same in our reading. It's not." Similarly, when non-romance readers claim that the genre is unrealistic, romance readers demand to know what is so unrealistic about love. No one is debating the realism of that cartoon hero with the eight-pack abs, or the violet-eyed heroine. What's at stake are realistic expectations for relationships. Love. Sex. These are high stakes indeed, because they can realistically affect our personal happiness and change the dynamics between people in a relationship. Especially if the couple is married or cohabitating, there can be financial implications or serious effects for the kids.

But did romance novels *give* readers these high expectations or just confirm that yes, it is reasonable to expect *more* from your partner? My hunch is that romances tap into an instinctive need for, you know, *partnering* from one's partner and reinforce that it's perfectly normal to crave sex, conversation, intimacy, and socks in the hamper. It is perfectly normal to want someone you love to take care of themselves so they can be around for more loving. Because romance novels make readers feel that their desires are normal and reasonable and give them an image in their mind to aspire to, perhaps they will hold out for a reality that delivers what they want. They can change or make changes.

Dismissing the books as unrealistic is a way to lower expectations for relationships. It is a way for that porcine husband—or the emotional and physical sloth in a relationship, regardless of gender—to avoid the ghastly nightly aerobics, and it is a way to make those who wish for a more fulfilling relationship feel weird, wrong, or unreasonable for wanting that. But with every romance a person reads, she learns how damn good it feels to be nurtured, loved, pleasured, and respected. And she learns, hopefully, that her wishes, desires, and fantasies are perfectly valid.

Ugh, girl stuff

Dismissing romance novels is a way of dismissing women. For all the gains women have made—they now have more of a voice and role in public life and the right to vote, own property, have a credit card in their name, make choices regarding their own body, and get an education—there is still a stigma about girl things, whether it's pink stuff, princesses, "female" industries, or romance novels.

Women live in a world built for men, from the social structures that position man as the authority to air bags designed to protect a person the size of the average male— and not the average female. In contrast, romance novels are a world created for women to confirm and validate their experiences, points of view, and desires. This may make it unrealistic for some people, but not for all.

And it matters that women should be able to find a fictional world built to serve and reflect their needs, their desires, and their hopes and to validate their experiences.

Contemporary romance author Jennifer Crusie says it best on her blog:

The world that romance fiction has shown me is more real than anything most of the literary canon ever offered me. Most of my academic reading convinced me that fiction reflected male worlds told by male authorities. But once I read romance, I found that even the most abysmal examples of the genre took place in my world, a world of relationships, details, and victories that balanced my defeats. Better than that, the best of the genre often directly contradicted patriarchal common wisdom by re-visioning the male assumptions I'd grown up reading, telling me that my perceptions were valid after all. Romance fiction was reality fiction.[13]

———

IN A KNEE-JERK REACTION to claims that romances are unrealistic, romance readers can retort "Oh no, they're not!" but that is forgetting that these books *are fantasy*. The characters and actions are highly idealized—and that is precisely why these books are so powerful. Women create an idealized, hopeful vision for the future to inspire other women. Fiction and fantasy are the crucial first steps to changing the world.

Declaring these books unrealistic is a way to blunt their power. A snide remark of "Oh, you don't really believe that, do you?" is a way to make a reader question not just her reading material but also herself and her hopes for the future. To dismiss these books as unrealistic is a way to try to make them so.

WHO IS THE ROMANCE NOVEL READER?

READERSHIP

MALE

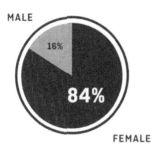

16%

84%

FEMALE

59% live with a spouse or significant other

70% of readers discover the genre between the ages of 11-18*

The U.S. romance book buyer is most likely to be aged between

30 and 54 years.

TOP REASONS TO READ ROMANCE

ENTERTAINMENT

ESCAPE

RELAXATION*

(and because they make her happy)

Romance book buyers are highly represented in the

SOUTH.

60% consider themselves feminists*

35% buy romance novels more than once a month

 **AVERAGE INCOME**
$55,000

THE STORY is the #1 factor in a reader's purchasing decision

Sources: Romance Writers of America, Nielsen Books and Consumer Tracker. http://bit.ly/1EIPm1S. *The Dangerous Books For Girls Survey.

EIGHT

WHAT WE TALK ABOUT WHEN WE TALK ABOUT BODICE RIPPERS

He let her go, ripped open her wrapper, and tore her corset
down to her waist.
　　—*Deadly Caresses* by Brenda Joyce

BODICE RIPPER IS a phrase that just won't die. It is also the phrase that is most likely to arouse the ire and inflame the passions of romance readers. "I think it's a pejorative term," says Jane Litte of the popular romance blog Dear Author. Many a romance reader would agree. One blogger even goes so far as to describe the term *bodice ripper* as the "the N-word of literature."[1] There is something about the phrase that seems insulting and even demeaning to readers. So why are we still using it?

Traditionally speaking, the phrase *bodice ripper* applies specifically to the long form historical romances of the 1970s, which are actually described quite well by the Urban Dictionary:

An historical romance where the heroine has lots of nonconsensual sex, which becomes consensual. The book needs to have a gaudy cover with a woman with an extraordinarily long neck, heaving bosoms, and flowing hair and a brooding man.

Technically, the phrase should really just apply to the romances of the 1970s—*Sweet Savage Love, The Flame and the Flower,* and so on—however, unfortunately, it persists. But romances aren't like that anymore, as Eloisa James points out in her *New York Times* op-ed: "These days, however, a romance heroine is likely to toss her own bra, and if buttons are skittering on the floor, they're quite possibly shirt studs."[2] (Though I did recently read a scene from a book published in 2003 where the hero literally ripped the heroine's corset *and* drawers and then—well, you know what then. I should note that it was very, very consensual.[3]).

But still: Why, why, why in the era of no means no, yes means yes, and society actively fighting rape culture, are we still laughingly using a phrase that implies women need to be forced into sex or enjoy rapey sex—and love to read about it for entertainment?

The reason is that as a culture, women's desire and sexuality still freaks us out. We're fine with a girl on the cover of *Sports Illustrated* magazine, shoving her bikini bottom down so low it seems like her vagina has been airbrushed out.[4] But the minute a major motion picture shows a woman receiving oral sex, the Motion Picture Association of America freaks out and forces changes.

Elyse Discher, a reviewer at Smart Bitches, Trashy Books, tells me, "If I have come to one conclusion as an adult, it's that a healthy depiction of a woman enjoying her sexuality is the most scandalous thing on earth ever." And many romance novels have come to provide healthy depictions of female sexuality. Not that we would know it, the way the conversation is always about bodice rippers with the implication that women don't want sex unless a man makes them want it.

But a real conversation about bodice rippers and romance novels cannot be had without talking about women's sexuality and pleasure. It's the sex talk everyone, even grown-ups, are afraid to have.

AFTER SPENDING hundreds of millions of dollars in search of a female Viagra, most drug manufacturers have given up. Which is a pity for their bottom line and perhaps a pity for the estimated 40 to 45 percent[5] of women who suffer from female sexual dysfunction. For women, sexual arousal isn't just a simple matter of blood flow. Women can become physically aroused in terms of blood flow to their lady parts, but that doesn't mean they're psychologically aroused. In the immortal words of Madonna, "he needs to start with your head."

It's even more complicated than that, according to Dr. Louann Brizendine, M.D., a neuropsychiatrist: "female sexual turn-on begins, ironically, with a brain turnoff." A woman has to feel safe and worry free, so the amygdala—the fear and anxiety portion of the brain—shuts down. Her feet have to be warm.[6] That's a lot for one little pill to accomplish. Or a human.

Women's sexuality and desire is complicated. There are extra steps. But not in a bodice ripper. Most romance scholars and readers agree that to understand the sexuality in these books, one must understand the context in which they were written and read. While the Middle Ages fretted over women's insatiable sexual appetites, in the eighteenth and nineteenth century, we saw the opposite view take over. It became generally accepted that "women weren't troubled by sexual feelings of any kind."[7] Thanks to the sexual revolution that kicked off in the 1960s, the advent of the pill, and dramatically changing roles for females, women were finally about to explore this aspect of themselves. But where to begin?

Collectively, women were stepping out in a major way and it was uncharted territory. Bestselling author Eloisa James explains, "all of a sudden you're going to work, you're supposed to be handling the sexual revolution, having orgasms, doing all this stuff." This is when the bodice rippers hit the bookshelves, just in time to help women try to make sense of it all. In these books "the guy would hold her down and she could experience sexual pleasure without having to work for it and without having to say yes," James notes. While many women would have been happy to "work" for the pleasure, they probably didn't have much knowledge or experience of how to get the job done. In these books, a woman could explore sexual desire without the guilt and shame of asking for it, whatever "it" might be. The heroine could still have the sex she secretly, privately, wanted to have, but without the stigma of having requesting or initiating it (slut shaming is still a problem *now*; imagine what it must have been like over 40 years ago). The hero's job, then, was to make her confront the desire she felt.

As our culture has become more accepting of women's sexuality and desire—and yes, we have—we've seen a change in the sexual dynamics between the couple in a romance novel. *Sweet Savage Love,* perhaps the bodice rippiest of the bodice rippers, includes many moments like this:

She had forced herself to be prepared for a quick, brutal rape, but instead, against her will and the silent, screaming protest of her mind, her body, vital and young, was beginning to respond to his caresses.[8]

In comparison, consider *Fifty Shades of Grey*, which to some is an open and shut case of Man Dominates Woman. But they spend *the entire book negotiating what they'll do in bed.* She sets hard limits. He respects them and says "You don't have to do anything you don't want to do." Anastasia is open and not conflicted about her desire for him. The reader does have to listen to a bit of rationalization and justification from her Inner Goddess for sleeping with the hot, kinky billionaire, but her exploration isn't forced.

And that's just one example of how the genre has changed. Long before #YesMeansYes, a trending hashtag on Twitter and the informal term for new laws that make affirmative consent central to school sexual assault policies,[9] romance novelists began adding a little something to their sex scenes: explicit consent. The hero and heroine are getting it on and we're in her point of view, so we know she's really wants it and the hero is hard, at her entrance, and dying for this pleasure, and still they take a moment to confirm that, yes, this is totally hot and everyone agrees it should go further. For example, there is this exchange in Tessa Dare's novel *Say Yes to the Marquess,* which I selected because it was literally the last romance novel I read, as of this writing, thus demonstrating how easy it is to find these examples:

He took his cock in hand and positioned himself at her entrance. "Tell me you want this."

"I want this."

Gritting his teeth, he teased them both by sliding the tip of his erection in, then out. "Tell me you want me."

Her eyes opened and locked with his. "Rafe. I want you. Only you."

These days, heroines embark on sexual relations with both eyes open and far more knowledge about and acceptance of their own desires. Even in historical romances where, strictly speaking, the heroine would probably have very little knowledge about the mechanics of sex before her wedding night and presumably would never have masturbated, we now see historical heroines portraying more honest and open knowledge about sex. The heroine of *Say Yes to the Marquess* is not ignorant about how to give herself pleasure. The heroine of *Unraveled,* a historical romance by Courtney Milan, uses a sponge system to prevent pregnancy—in nineteenth century England.

And yet, in advance of the launch of the *Fifty Shades of Grey* movie, there were conversations about how much sex should be shown—and how much, ahem, of the actor people want to see. That we even discuss this shows an assumption that women aren't interested in seeing much nudity (especially if it's of the male variety) or graphic sex scenes on the big screen. Why is this even a question? Why wouldn't women be interested in sex? Why wouldn't we be interested in sex in romantic entertainment? How many copies does E. L. James have to sell before we stopped being surprised by women wanting sex?

THE TRUTH IS: We're not surprised by women's sexual desire. We're *terrified* of it. We don't always understand it or how it works, and it's not always clear where the line is between aroused and annoyed, sexy "throw down" or rape, and good god, what do *feelings* have to do with it all? Where is the goddamn clitoris and/or the G spot anyway? We know, in our heart of hearts, that it's more complicated than insert tab A into slot B. And "bodice ripping" is a way to reduce the complexity. It's a way to cut off the knot of emotion and raw, unfiltered sexual desire rather than attempt to untangle it.

Talking about bodice rippers, in which anxieties are ruthlessly ripped and shoved aside, is a way to avoid talking about the complexity of female desire and sexual experience. And we *really, really* don't want to have this conversation. We don't want to have it in schools, which is why we have abstinence education instead of sexual education. When conservatives rail against female birth control, it's often out of concern that it leads to promiscuity, to which the other side replies that it's used to treat a variety of conditions, many not sexually related. But both operate on the assumption that it's *wrong* for women to be having lots of sex, especially for nonprocreative purposes.

We see it in the UK ban on certain acts in pornography. Video on Demand porn and DVD sex-shop porn are no longer allowed to show content featuring, among other things, spanking, physical restraint, or female ejaculation. Um, hello? Are these lawmakers not aware of what women are reading in books purchased at their local supermarket, right next to the milk and eggs?!

We see a fear of women's sexuality in the practice of female genital mutilation, in which the clitoris—the source of female orgasm—is cut off. Rather than even discuss female desire, they try to get rid of it completely. While this is predominantly a practice in African and Middle Eastern cultures, this isn't just practiced in a land far, far away: "The number of women and girls in the United States at risk of female genital mutilation has more than doubled since 2000 to half a million, say demographic researchers who expect that figure to rise even further."[10]

We would like to think that women don't want to do all these naughty, kinky things. We would like to think they still aren't troubled by sexual feelings or that they certainly don't need birth control. We would prefer to think that if a woman has sex, it's because some man made her do it. Meanwhile, romance is a billion dollar industry, erotica is one of the fastest growing categories, and *Fifty Shades of Grey* has sold *a hundred million copies.*

Romance authors and readers are not afraid to revel in those grey areas of powerful emotions, potent desire, and the unfiltered exploration of both. Rather than simplify, the more complicated and twisted, the better. Does she hate him but want his body so bad? Yes! Has he sworn never to love again, but cannot stop himself from wanting to bury himself inside her? *Yes!* Is this love and desire forbidden? YES! Complications are hot and sexy. Resolving them is fucking fantastic.

But that's too much for some people, who feel more comfortable with a simple and classic understanding of sex between men and women: She's a coy female and he knows what to do. Turgid Tab A goes into Female Slot B and they live happily ever after.

But aren't we past all that? Don't we know better? Yes. And it's *hard* knowing better. It's especially tempting to continue to evoke bodice rippers and their simplified presentation of sexuality, given the news these days. When brutal rapes are in the headlines too damn much, laughing about bodice rippers is a way to suggest that maybe she liked it and maybe she really wanted it without, you know, actually saying it. Maybe it's not the end of this girl's life as she knows it (or, wah wah, the boy rapists). Maybe it's the beginning of a beautiful relationship. Maybe they can still live happily ever after.

When we talk about bodice rippers, we are acknowledging that sexuality, particularly female pleasure, scares us, and that we prefer to ignore it. We are demonstrating that we are more comfortable with a paradigm of sexuality that reduces a woman to a passive, ignorant body and a man to a tool even though it probably leaves a lot of people sexually and emotionally unsatisfied.

NINE

PURE HEROINE

FROM "OH NO" TO "OH YES"

WOMEN'S SEXUALITY has been endlessly discussed, often by men, and often by celibate men at that. Too often, the options presented are extreme opposites: She must be a virgin or a whore; she is innocent and good and has all the potential in the world, or she is ruined, bad, and useless. She has voracious sexual appetites or no sexual feeling at all.

Romance novels are the space where women can examine their sexuality on their own terms. And while there are plenty of trembling virgins and hard heroes who show them what they're missing, these books present an alternative view—one that isn't either/or, black/white, but one with shades of grey.

The virgin heroine: WTF?

Nothing highlights the importance of virginity in romance quite like the virgin widow trope. In these particular plots, the heroine has managed to go through a marriage (for years, in some instances) without having had sex with her husband. This is often due to impotent old men, absent husbands, or kindly old men who just want to marry a very young girl to not have sex with, but to grant her access to his impressive library (there is *so* much to unpack in that fantasy).

The Virgin Widow has to be one of the most absurd tropes, and it leads one to wonder *why* authors go to such great lengths to preserve a heroine's virginity throughout a marriage.

Part of the reason is because romance novels reflect the world in which they are written and read. In real life, for most of human history, a woman's sole value was in her marriage-ability, which was dependent upon her virginity, because we developed a system of private property that relied almost entirely on the paternity of offspring. A woman's virginity was a way to ensure a man's kids were his and that his wealth was passed on appropriately. A woman's virginity became her primary possession and currency in a world that did not allow women to legally own anything. Virginity was the one bargaining chip a woman had to cash in or exchange for better circumstances.

In many places in the world, it still is.

Many eighteenth and nineteenth century novels for women tended to emphasize the virtue of the heroine (Exhibit A, the bestseller *Pamela; Or, Virtue Rewarded*). And many historical romance plots hinge on a heroine's sexual inexperi-ence—for example, a marriage of convenience to protect her reputation, a heroine who deliberately gets "ruined" by a notorious rake to avoid an unwanted marriage, or a couple caught in a compromising position and swiftly marched down the aisle.

Like virtuous women in real life, books with virtuous heroines were deemed acceptable for polite company. While there was a great fear that novels would corrupt innocent young women, a heroine who exemplified virtuous behavior made a book more suitable. This also widened the audience for the books, and thus the potential market and sales. Books deemed "unsuitable for ladies were commercially sunk."[1] Virtuous, virginal heroines—like virtuous, virginal women—were worth something.

Virginity, then, was all about value. For a real life woman, it was what she could trade for a better life and marriage and thus a measure of economic security. Or at the very least, by preserving it, she could avoid becoming a "fallen woman," potentially with a child to support and barely any way to financially support herself—an economic disaster for herself and the community that would have to support them. The linking of virginity and marriage, then, wasn't just some lofty, noble, ideal but a practical consideration. In *Virgin: The Untouched History,* author Hanne Blank writes of the Middle Ages: "Spinsters and bachelors were as rare as hen's teeth. Remaining unmarried was not an option many would, or could, choose. Economic survival meant participation in the economy of the larger household and community."[2] This pressure only increased with the Industrial Revolution.

But the funny thing about physical virginity is that it doesn't really exist. "Virginity cannot be seen or measured, in and of itself," Blank writes in book that explores historical, medical, and religious concepts of virginity. What she found is that there isn't really a physical, medical, reliably testable way to establish a woman's sexual state. "Virginity tests do not look for virginity, but for signs of virginity. The difference is subtle but crucial," she writes. "Virginity tests cannot tell us whether an individual woman is a virgin; they can only tell us whether or not she conforms to what people of her time and place believe to be true of virgins."[3]

That, of course, assumes that virginity ends with penis-into-vagina sex. How far in does it have to go? But what about anal sex? What about oral sex? Studies show that teenagers who took virginity pledges were more likely to engage in anal and oral sex. And how does it all apply to gays and lesbians? Are there separate virginities, some more valuable than others?

What the Virgin Widow plot does is separate sex from marriage. Traditionally, because she presumably no longer had virginity or value to protect, a widowed woman had more freedom to travel unaccompanied in the world or have a gentleman caller without a chaperone breathing down their necks.

Why not just have a widow, then? Because the romance heroine's virgin state isn't purely about whether or not she's had sex. It's not because romance writers are reinforcing ideas that only virgins have value, or that heroes care about a woman's level of sexual experience and want to be her first, last, and only. The romance heroine's virginity signifies the un-awakened woman.

And romance is about a woman waking up.

The rude awakening

All these frantic thoughts buzzed in a small, secret part of her. It was the same place where she hid the core of her self —the shining rainbow of her mind. Layered in multiple shields she continually reinforced, it couldn't be breached by anyone without using such brutal force that it would kill her.

————*Slave to Sensation* by Nalini Singh

In *Sleeping Beauty,* the awakening begins with just a kiss. It's a gentle version of what we see again and again in romance novels, where the hero often takes charge of the heroine's sexual awakening. He's the guide through which she discovers her own desire, explores her sexuality, and emerges on the other side as an experienced woman with a deeper knowledge of her body and herself.

If romances are stories of a woman's sexual awakening, then the rape of the bodice rippers or the forced seductions of other later books are rude awakenings, indeed. But they also served a purpose. "Women are taught to be ashamed if they're horny, to be ashamed if they own their sexuality; if someone is sexually aggressive, they're a slut," says Sarah Wendell of the blog Smart Bitches, Trashy Books. "There's a lot of negativity. The forced seduction allowed them to experience arousal but not feel any guilt for having initiated it."

The bodice ripper functioned as part of that awakening for the real-life woman. In her book *When Everything Changed: The Amazing Journey of American Women from 1960 to the Present*, Gail Collins writes, "American society had always given women only one big responsibility when it came to sex —stopping boyfriends from going too far. Now [the 1970s] they seemed to be in charge of everything, from providing the birth control to making sure they had orgasms. A great deal of research was required."[4] While there were workshops and classes, research could be had cheaply, easily, and privately via a mass-market paperback novel that a woman could slip into her grocery cart. (This is especially crucial given that women weren't legally granted the right to have credit cards in their own names until 1974.[5])

"The sexual revolution was about more than whether women should be able to feel as free as men to have sex before marriage," Collins writes. "It was also about whether women—single or married—had as much right to enjoy sex."[6] The romance novel said yes.

Nothing to lose but her chains...and a world to win

I've been afraid of my own voracious appetites, tamping
myself down, shying away from my own power.
    —*Roulette* by Megan Mulry

If we are still operating with the assumption that virginity =
value and it's only good to redeem for marriage, then the
destruction or removal of that value opens up entire worlds to
the heroine. "Freedom's just another word for nothing left to
lose," Janis Joplin sang. When a heroine is no longer
preserving her virginity for the Noble Life Goal of Marriage,
she is at liberty to do whatever the hell she wants. But what
does she want to do?

Again, it's probably not a coincidence that these sexually
explicit stories appeared when they did, during the sexual
revolution and women's movement, when women were stepping out into the workplace. For the first time, it became
acceptable to have aspirations other than marriage. Collins
writes, "It was in the 1970s that American women set off on a
new course. They went to college thinking about what work
they wanted to do, not what man they wanted to catch, and
flooded professional schools with applications. After gradua-
tion, they no longer marched right off to the altar, and the
median age of marriage rose rather dramatically." Romance
novels are about a heroine achieving a deeper understanding
of herself—and that includes her sexual self—as well as
finding what gives her life meaning and value. In order to
embark on that journey and find her place in a new world, we
needed to get rid of pesky assumptions, rules, and expectations that keep women tethered to the old order. We had to

devalue the idea of virginity and break its association with marriage.

And we did. Attitudes in real life *and* fiction have shifted. "In contemporary romance, you're not seeing that many virgin heroines," says Tessa Woodward, the Avon editor. "And if they are, it's because they had some sort of block that the hero is going to help them through." Virginity is no longer a prerequisite for love or a determination of a woman's personal value.

Even in historical romances written today, when authors are obligated to represent these older values of a woman's virginity and marriageability, we now see clever plotting that subverts these rules while still being true to the time period. It's most apparent in stories of "fallen" women finding love, respect, and acceptance even though they are supposedly "ruined." In *Not Quite a Lady* by Loretta Chase, the heroine becomes an expert in "Not Getting Married" so no one will discover that she's not a virgin. Or in my own book, *What a Wallflower Wants*, the heroine learns to love, trust, and value herself after being raped by someone other than the hero.

Looking at paranormal romances, the concept of virginity and the forced removal of it is presented in slightly different ways, but it still reinforces the idea that these stories are truly about a character waking up to their full potential, or a different potential than one they'd grown up expecting.

Wendell notes that in paranormal romances, instead of the violation being forced upon the heroine's physical body, it's forced on her will: "This sort of metaphorical breach is especially pervasive in paranormal romances, in which heroines are often changed or transformed without their consent, even against their express wishes, by the hero."[7] One day she's just a girl, and the next she's a vampire, werewolf, or whatever other fantastical creature imaginative authors have invented.

Her life has been drastically altered, and there is no going back.

Eloisa James provides an interesting interpretation of this when it comes to vampire novels. "When you find your vampire bride, all of a sudden, your heart starts beating, all of a sudden, you're seeing in color, all of a sudden, you can taste food again." Talk about waking up.

The new awakening

> For a long moment there was only the sound of her soft, half-gasping little breaths, and the thud of his heart, loud in his ears. He had never felt this...this liberation, this unfettered contentment. Not with another woman, not after a hard day of accomplishment, not after a brilliant business maneuver, not even after beating his brothers at anything. His body was wrung out with physical satisfaction, his mind felt fogged and sluggish, but his head...
>
> "If this be madness," came Francesca's weak voice from behind the shining veil of her hair, "lead me to Bedlam."
>
> "Perhaps tomorrow. I don't think I can make it further than the bed."
>
> —One Night in London by Caroline Linden

Virginity is no longer a Big Deal in most romances—only 1 percent of readers said heroines should be virgins. These days, when heroines are willing or even eager to be divested of their virginity, do we still have "an awakening" of the heroine? We do, and we see an awakening of the hero now, too.

The orgasm may be the new awakening, as even sexually

experienced characters may not have had an orgasm with previous partners.

It is a very rare romance novel sex scene that doesn't have one, both, or all members of the scene climaxing at least once after demonstrating what and how and when it's achieved. The sex scene now is about the anticipation and discovery of pleasure and reveling in it every step of the way. Even when characters don't have spectacular sex together the first time, there is a still an intimate—and in its own way—pleasurable process of mutual discovery. Even when a character is "forced" to orgasm in romances portraying dominant and submissive role-playing, the character consents to it and anticipates it.

When the level of experience between the hero and heroine is uneven, authors still find ways to portray the awakening for both characters. The less experienced character may lie there, gasping for breath and whisper, "I had *no idea.*" Eyes have been opened not just to a new, fun way to pass the time but to the pleasure one can get from an erotic, emotional sexual encounter.

The more experienced character will lie there, gasping for breath and whisper, "It's never been like this before." Elle Keck, an editorial assistant at Avon, with the long blonde hair of a classic romance heroine, says it's a way of demonstrating "this is why this is special." The connection is deeper, the experience more profound because of the person it's done with.

And when it's the hero who says to the woman, in Keck's words, "out of all the women...you're the best," it's not just a compliment. What a profound shift that presents: A woman's value is not lost with participation in a sexual act. In fact, she is now *more special and more valuable.*

Ruined or revered?

Charlotte was a week shy of seventeen when her life changed, falling into two halves like a shiny child's ball: before *and* after.

—*Potent Pleasures* by Eloisa James

In *Potent Pleasures* by Eloisa James the dividing line between *before* and *after* is sex and there are major implications for crossing that line—as well as in real life. Our culture's sexual paradigms are built on an either/or dichotomy. A woman is either a virgin or a whore, a prude or a slut. We are valued for our sexual "purity" until we lose it; then a woman is valuable only for sex, and then only as a commodity, not as a person.

In her book *The Purity Myth: How America's Obsession with Virginity Is Hurting Young Women*, Jessica Valenti writes, "The lie of virginity—if such a thing even exists—is ensuring that young women's perception of themselves is inextricable from their bodies, and that their ability to be moral actors is absolutely dependent on their sexuality."

We see this in portrayals of female sexuality in literary fiction, when the sexually "transgressive" heroine dies in the type of horrible death reserved for villains. Madame Bovary's self-inflicted death by arsenic poisoning caused an uproar when it was published because it wasn't gruesome enough.

The fates of so many heroines of literary fiction send the message that sex = death: Juliet, Anna Karenina, Clarissa Harlowe, Catherine Earnshaw, and Edna Pontellier. Hester Prynne lived, but only as a cautionary tale and an example of seventeenth century slut shaming. Readers like to see emotional justice, in which the good are rewarded with a lifetime of happiness and the baddies are punished, usually with death. The message is obvious. Stories that dared to present an optimistic view of female sexuality, like *Fanny Hill: Memoirs of a Woman of Pleasure* or *Lady Chatterley's Lover*, were banned for obscenity, making these books—and their heroines—worthless.

But a romance heroine does not lose heroine status once she has sex. In fact, she is rewarded with a happy ending that consists of personal acceptance, love, and respect. The only thing that changes as a result of her sexual activity is that she now has more orgasms, a fuller knowledge of herself, and a deeper connection with the person she loves.

This is one reason romance novels are so revolutionary: They break the association between a woman's value and her level of sexual experience. They take back control and put it in her hands. And these books provide a satisfying alternative to the idea that a woman is either a virgin or a whore. She can just be her own woman.

TEN

LADY PORN

TRY THIS EXPERIMENT AT HOME: Leave a romance novel out in a public-ish place. Wait for someone to pick it up and flip through looking for the sex scenes to dramatically read aloud. I bet you won't be waiting long.

Romance novels are known for the smutty parts, the naughty bits, the cheap and easy thrills they provide. Never mind that romance novels come in a variety of "heat" levels, ranging from mild, hot, and scorcher, or from chaste inspirationals to stuff that makes *Fifty Shades of Grey* seem like child's play. Despite this range, the genre is still often reduced to just "porn for women."

This suggestion can give some people the vapors (pornography!), others get their unmentionables in a twist (it is so much more than that!), and others smile knowingly and say "oh hell, yes." Smart Bitches, Trashy Books blogger Sarah Wendell points out, "Romance is not porn for women. Porn is porn for women. There is nothing wrong with either one."[1]

But let's leave aside debates of "what is porn?" or "are romance novels porn?" or "what is male porn and what is female porn?" and focus on the fact that women are interested in reading about sex as it is portrayed in romance novels. In a big, billion-dollar way. While there is a growing trend of video pornography by women, for women, it still doesn't have the reach that romance novels do. Only one is in Walmart (but shhh—don't tell them!).

Whether we define these books as lady porn or not, the sex scenes have a big impact on how the genre is perceived. Sixty-three percent of survey respondents think the sexy bits contribute to the bad reputation of romance. "I think if there was no sexual content then they wouldn't be vilified to the extent that they are," says Jane Litte of the blog Dear Author. Two subjects simply fraught with angst and tension are porn and women's sexuality. Romances don't exactly shy away from either.

While some regular romance readers skip past these parts (too repetitive) and others prefer straight up erotica, most romance readers enjoy reading stories where the sexual component is a large part of the story and the development of the characters. It serves women's sexual needs from education and experimentation to escape and just plain pleasure.

The female sexuality portrayed in romance novels is also insanely different from almost every other portrayal out there. For one thing, "the female-to-male ratio of orgasms is always more skewed to women," points out Avon editorial assistant Elle Keck. This is the space where women, unmediated or censored, can explore all different aspects of their own sexuality, in their own voice and on their own terms.

Keyword: explore. Not: perform. So much of female sexuality is a glittery show to turn men on and sell products. "There is...ample evidence that the more mainstream media girls consume, the more importance they place on being sexy,"[2] Peggy Orenstein writes in her book *Cinderella Ate My Daughter*. This doesn't make them feel good; in fact, they report more depression and less ambition.

This pressure to perform sexiness has even more consequences. Orenstein cites the work of Stephen Hinshaw, chair of the Department of Psychology of UCLA, in explaining how damaging performing sex for other people can be: "Girls pushed to be sexy too soon can't really understand what they're doing...they do not—and may never—learn to connect their performance to erotic feelings or intimacy. They learn how to act desirable but not how to desire."

Romance novels flip the script by focusing extensively on how it feels for the woman. In fact, the focus is on the pleasure a female *feels*, not just from her partner's touch but also from the entire experience with a lover. They tend to focus on the hero's pride in pleasing the heroine: "The books often point out that he loved seeing the pleasure on her face," says Keck. His triumph is not from getting laid, but getting her off. Really good sex scenes in romances focus on emotions the characters are experiencing just as much, if not more, than the physical descriptions of the act.

The Sex Talk

Around the ages of 11 to 13, puberty is starting to hit, bodies are starting to change, and adolescents start to become aware of sex. Naturally, they have questions, but getting answers isn't easy.

The Daily Show hilariously exposes this in a segment called "Sin City's Missing Sex Education,"[3] which featured interviews with students in Las Vegas who were pressing for sex ed in their schools so they can make "healthy, educated decisions about their own bodies" and with Susan Patton, "The Princeton Mom," who thinks sex education should be taught by parents to their children. "They may not be experts but they can speak from their own experience," she says.

But when kids' questions about the transmission of STIs were posed to her, Patton admitted she didn't know the answer. Her response: Google it.

Coincidentally or not, 11 to 13 is also the age when a majority of romance readers (41 percent) discover the genre. Some readers don't quite pick up on the sexy stuff happening early on; it is only later that it dawns on them what was happening (all those euphemisms!). But for many teens—and grown women—romance novels provide a safe, nonjudgmental way to learn about sex.

Because romance novels have thus far frequently featured virgin heroines, the reader can learn along with her, like a trusted best friend or older sister who has an experience first and reports back. "She represents me when I was young and discovering all these things," says Maddie Caldwell, the leader of a Brooklyn-based romance book club. "She was learning about sex. I learned with her. She was my avatar."

This is not to say that romance novels take a moment to share information on how to prevent the spread of HPV or pregnancy, though in contemporary romance novels, it is highly unusual to see unprotected sex; there is at least a passing reference to ripping foil or a momentary pause while he puts a condom on. Romance novels are also guilty of perpetuating false information about the location of the hymen or how easy it is to achieve simultaneous orgasm with your partner through penetrative sex (though I would argue that we're getting better at providing more accurate and still sexy scenes).

What romance novels can teach readers about is the

mechanics of sex and how to make sex pleasurable. They also teach about arousal.

"The female reading it is learning what turns her on. And that's empowering," says Sarah Wendell. "So even if you have a narrative that is very stereotypical, you still have the reader experiencing arousal and figuring out 'okay, I like these scenes but I don't like those scenes and now I understand my own sexuality based on what I'm reading.'"

When so much sex education directed to women (and men!) is "overwhelmingly negative and both condemnatory and keeping them in ignorance," as Wendell says, romance novels are a way to explore different scenarios in a safe, nonjudgmental manner. The only risk is perhaps the 99 cents you paid for the e-book.

And then there is the sheer quantity of romance novels and diversity of sexuality presented. There is something for everyone, from "vanilla sex" to BDSM and beyond. "One of the things that I think was good about *50 Shades* is that it made the idea of sexual role play something that everyone understood was a thing that was happening," Wendell says. "This is a thing that people do and it's okay to be turned on." And that is just one book. There is undoubtedly a romance novel for every desire.

Great sexplorations

The comedian Louis CK tells a joke about the different acts of courage in dating. When men go on a date, their big courageous act is asking out a woman. For the woman, it's saying yes. "A woman saying yes to a date with a man is literally insane and ill advised...when you consider that there is no greater threat to women than men."

It's funny because it's true. It is not safe out there for a woman because Men. We tell women to carry mace and rape whistles and to curtail their movements so as to avoid dangerous situations. If women do go on a date, many text a friend when they're home safe. We have a buddy system for dating! It's tricky out there for gays and lesbians as well; it was (and in some parts of the world still is) a crime punishable by death to explore those sexual desires. And that is to say nothing of the risk of STDS for all parties involved, and unintended pregnancies. Or soul-crushing rejection, mortification, and failure.

Sex is risky. That's part of what makes it so thrilling.

But in romance novels, readers can explore a variety of sexual desires and practices in the safety and privacy of their own home, with no consequences and very little risk. "The reader can live vicariously through the heroine and fall in love with the hero, but without any of the consequences," says Maryanne Fisher, PhD, in an article for *Psychology Today*.[4] "She's not cheating on her husband (most readers are married) because it's just a novel. She isn't at risk of becoming pregnant, but she can imagine the seduction by the hero. She gets the thrill, the rush of falling in love—all for a few dollars."

Studies have shown that when we read, the experience in our brain is more involved than originally thought, as *The New York Times* reports:

Researchers have long known that the "classical" language regions, like Broca's area and Wernicke's area, are involved in how the brain interprets written words. What scientists have come to realize in the last few years is that narratives activate many other parts of our brains as well, suggesting why the experience of reading can feel so alive. Words like "lavender," "cinnamon" and "soap," for example, elicit a response not only from the language-processing areas of our brains, but also those devoted to dealing with smells.

While the article and the study did not mention reading erotica, it might not be a leap to conclude that all those sensory words and descriptions of action and feeling are lighting up the brain all over. In short, "The brain, it seems, does not make much of a distinction between reading about an experience and encountering it in real life; in each case, the same neurological regions are stimulated."

So what, then, does that say about women reading romances with scenes of forced seduction? Or what about the rise of the BDSM romance, with its often male-dominant and female-submissive scenarios? Do women really want to be raped and dominated?

Not necessarily, but that's not to discount readers who do have rape fantasies. "The thing about a rape fantasy is that you are consenting from the beginning," says Wendell. "The fear and other aspects of that situation are erotic to you. There is an undercurrent of empowerment in deciding to participate willingly in that scenario. If that's what floats your boat, that's fine."

Recently, the big trend has been the BDSM fantasy, as exemplified by *Fifty Shades of Grey,* and the explosion of similarly themed erotica in its wake (however respectfully or accurately it may or may not be depicted). "I do think BDSM romance is the new rape book," says Maddie Caldwell. "And not in a bad way."

There's more at work here than a yearning for spanking and new accessories to shop for. Jane Litte, of Dear Author, explains the deeper appeal:

One of the reasons I think BDSM is such a popular subtrope of romance is because those books really talk about the power exchange, which I think is an inherently interesting issue for women because it's something we deal with every day. They really explore the emotional idea of trust and partnership. The idea of permission. The idea you can trust the partner with anything.

Can a real-life woman trust this man enough to say yes to a date with him, at night, with wine? Can a woman have enough trust to bare her body (which probably doesn't look like the ones on TV), risking her physical safety or emotional security? Or, hell, can a woman trust a boss not to judge her differently because she's a woman, or can she count on her partner to take the trash out? We all know the everyday version of trust; in romance, we can explore it, experiment, learn what it feels like by reading about it, often in far more sexy context.

As with the hero who knows just what the heroine wants, even if she doesn't know it herself, the BDSM hero's goal "is to bring you pleasure even if you're afraid to go there, or you don't know what's on the other side," as Litte says.

It should be noted that not all BDSM doms in romance novels are men or billionaires or heterosexual. The heroine isn't always the submissive either. The novel *Bound to Be a Groom* by Megan Mulry depicts a heroine who loves being in charge with a hero who likes taking orders. The novel *The Siren* by Tiffany Reisz depicts a heroine who is an erotica author, one of the only female doms at an S&M club, and who teaches her editor that he likes to submit.

Lust and...

For all the talk of porn, pleasure, heaving bosoms, and turgid members, for many romance readers, the appeal of sex scenes is not just about the blow-by-blow description of the sex act(s). Only 28 percent found the graphic descriptions to be what makes love scenes sexy. Seventy-one percent find the emotions of the characters the sexiest part of a sex scene and 83 percent get most turned on by the tension between the characters.

And, I would add now, the tension within the characters as they struggle with desire, deny it, and finally surrender to it.

Brenda Chin, the editorial director at ImaJinn books and former Harlequin editor, eloquently explains how the sexual tension of the characters impacts the reader:

You have to have a great buildup of sexual tension between the characters. Sexual tension comes from characterization. It must be spot on and we have to identify immediately with the heroine. The reader needs to fall for the hero. We need to know that he's a good guy. And then we can sit back and watch. If the author puts a lot of sexual tension all the way through, by the time they get together, they're ready to burst and so are we.

Indeed, it's that ever-building sexual tension that makes the sex scenes so damn good, Sometimes it takes a few hundred pages to build up to the breaking point. The tension doesn't just come from beating hearts, breathless heroines, or blood flow—it's more than just physical. It's emotional.

"These BDSM stories tend to explore at a deeper emotional level the headspace of characters," says Jane Litte. "The idea is that it's an emotion based story, not a physically based one. Even though they're having sex repeatedly, it's as much about the emotional release as it is about the physical."

This applies to almost any romance novel and its sex scenes. Romance novels are predominantly written from both the hero and heroine's point of view, so we know what everyone is thinking and feeling, creating a rich, immersive experience. Talk about feeling all the feelings.

And this union of the emotional and sexual is another way that romance novels are set apart from other representations of sexuality. It's not about any one person getting off, but two people coming together (literally and figuratively, wink).

SEX SCENES IN ROMANCE NOVELS

What do you think makes for a really hot, sexy scene in a romance novel?

- **71%** The emotions of the characters
- **28%** Graphic descriptions of the sexual activity
- **83%** The sexual tension between the characters

What heat level do you prefer?

- **2%** Mild
- **13%** Medium
- **14%** Hot
- **6%** Spicy
- **62%** All of the above

Why do you think old skool romances included rape scenes?

- **35%** Women weren't "allowed" to ask for sex
- **46%** Women weren't "allowed" to desire sex
- **9%** Women want men to take control
- **26%** The idea that the hero is overcome with desire for the heroine is appealing
- **32%** I have no idea, these scenes are terrible
- **21%** I just don't know

When people say romance novels are just porn for women, what is your response?

- **40%** They are not!
- **31%** They are but they're so much more.
- **46%** Who cares if they are?

What readers said on the sexual experience of characters:

 **ONLY 1%** think heroines should be virgins

 **77%** says it depends on the story

I could care less if either character has had a ton of sex before they met each other or not.

If I am reading a Regency romance and the heroine is a spinster then yes, I prefer her to be (mostly) historically accurately inexperienced. In contemporary romance I don't care.

I don't want the stereotype of the blushing virgin or anything smacking of old-skoolness.

Are there virgin heroes?

Oh MAN, the feminist in me is screaming, but as I mentioned before I love it best when she's a virgin. Or at the least, of course has never felt SUCH passion.

Sometimes it's beautiful to read about a heroine who has been scarred in the past and the hero helps to give her a sexual reawakening.

Sexually experienced heroes are very cool and I have no issues with them. But virgin heroes are a rarely seen trope so I am never unhappy to see them.

It's more important that he LEARNS how to please the heroine.

I do NOT like for the hero to have had so much sex that he's noted for his sexual liaisons. Eww.

I like the ones who are shown to be paying attention to the woman as they make love to her.

What readers said about sex in romance novels:

I like lots of scenes where the hero restrains himself from doing anything so that the payoff is satisfying.

There has to be lots of juicy tension leading up to it.

But for goodness sake, save me from quivering members!

Pretty much don't read them.

It has to reveal something about the characters.

The seduction is hot.

Sex scenes are completely worthless to me if I don't genuinely feel the frustration and emotion between these two people.

Source: The Dangerous Books For Girls study

ELEVEN

THE REAL APPEAL OF THE ALPHA

THE ENDURING ATTRACTION OF A TROUBLING TROPE

ON MAY 23, 2014, Elliot Rodger went on a killing spree in Isla Vista, California. He was a mentally unstable and enraged 22-year-old virgin who had never been kissed. Much of his rage was directed at the women who never found him attractive and the men who got the girls, in spite of having less money and crappier cars. In his manifesto, he writes, "You will finally see that I am, in truth, the superior one. The true alpha male."

I shuddered when I read this because I thought of the thousands of romance novels with alpha male heroes written, read, and loved by millions of women. Even those who don't read romances often get the gist of the type of hero they so often portray: the duke, the sheik, the billionaire, the one who has it all and takes the girl, too. After all, Fabio isn't exactly posing gently with those cover girls.

Of course the term alpha isn't confined to just romances; it's a term to describe the individual in a community (not confined to humans) with the highest rank. But ever since Alan Boon of Mills & Boon decided that romances should adhere to "nature's law," which is the rule of the Alpha Man, who is "strong, brave, mentally and physically tough, intelligent, tall and dark," the romance genre has celebrated, romanticized, and even fetishized the idea of the alpha male hero.

Boon has long argued that "all women gravitate toward this type of man, and wimpish heroes are not successful,"[1] and book sales have proven him right. Unfortunately, science has disproven Boons' interpretation of evolutionary biology and the pervasive view that women are most interested in a man's material assets and men are interested in a woman's physical assets. "We have systematically destroyed that," says Eli Finkel, a professor of Social Psychology at Northwestern University, on a panel on the science of history of love at the popular romance conference in Washington, D.C.

In fact, Finkel tells us that science has confirmed the utterly unsurprising truth that "everybody likes people who are hot rather than people who are ugly. And everybody prefers people who have some amount of ambition and earning potential."

Many still buy into the outdated interpretation of men and women's sexual dynamics featuring the aggressive male and the coy female, and it leads to some confounding questions. Do women romanticize the patriarchy and get off on submission? Are we shallow creatures who care only for men with status, wealth, and power—never mind how they treat women?

"Why is it that romance readers can tolerate any number of crazed behaviors from a romance hero, whereas if a real-life dude did one-tenth of a hero's dastardly deeds, not the least of which is raping the heroine, she'd be calling 911 faster than you can say 'restraining order'?"[2] asks Sarah Wendell and Candy Tan in their book *Beyond Heaving Bosoms: The Smart Bitches Guide to Romance Novels.*

This is the point where many sigh, throw up their hands, and say "it's just fiction!" But not always. In real life, women are at greatest risk of harm and abuse from the men in their personal lives. Or in the case of Elliot Rodger, this notion of what a man *should* be and what women *should* want can lead to deranged and deadly behavior.

Alpha hero vs alphHole

> He's very driven, controlling, arrogant—scary, but very charismatic. I can understand the fascination.
> —*Fifty Shades of Grey* by E. L. James

First, a distinction must be made between an alpha hero and alphHole. The blog Heroes and Heartbreakers provides some concise definitions:

> **Alpha hero**: *A dominant, aggressive, hyper-masculine hero.*
>
> **AlphHole**: *A critical term for an Alpha Male hero whose aggressive, forceful behavior crosses the line from romantic to abusive. This can be a contentious issue in the romance community as one reader's "protective" can be another reader's "controlling." Often the line comes down to personal taste.*[3]

Where a particular hero falls on the spectrum depends, in large part, on the skills of the writer. Is this domineering hero paired with a woman who stands up to him or Miss Doormat who allows him to go too far? How much secret pain from a tortured past does he possess to justify his behavior? Can the author write him as a conflicted human with motivation or is he a one-dimensional character "showing" his alpha-ness by acting like an asshole and displaying, in the words of one reader, "way too much financial and physical clout"?

Readers are attuned to the shades of grey between different types of heroes. Responses to hero preferences were totally mixed in my survey: 21 percent love alpha heroes, 11 percent love beta heroes (simply defined as not alpha), 34 percent say it doesn't matter if it's written by a favorite author, and 32 percent replied that it all depends on their mood.

The popular perception says that women want the worst of the alphHole: the arrogance, the controlling behavior, the raping, the lack of emotional availability. But these are the qualities readers deplore in these heroes. Even those who love alphas often included comments like "but he can't be TOO alpha." What is sexy about a well-written alpha is his confidence, the way he stands up in disasters big and small, and the way he knows how to please a woman even if she doesn't know it herself. Yet.

The alpha hero's appeal endures. In the past few years, he's been toned down, certainly (the alpha hero: now with less rape and kidnapping!). Even though there are a lot of unmentionables in a twist over this kind of guy, here's why we love them.

The alpha hero nurtures a woman in a world that doesn't

> *The feeling of relinquishing responsibility to someone else, letting him take control, was a relief beyond words.*
> —*Sugar Daddy* by Lisa Kleypas

In *Fifty Shades of Grey*, Christian one-ups every man ever when it comes to taking Ana on a dinner date. He reserves a private room, orders her entrée and wine, and insists that she partake ("Eat, Anastasia."). Of course he arranged for her transportation, too. In contrast, I once had a job taking reservations for some fancy New York City restaurants and I can't tell you how many guys called up at the last minute, begging for a reservation, having forgotten their anniversary or their wife's birthday. Not to mention picking the right bottle of wine and flying her home in a helicopter to beat the traffic.

Alpha behavior can sometimes go too far with "forced comfort" or creepy, controlling behavior. But when done right, it's also kind of...nurturing. Nurturing on steroids, to be sure, but this is fiction. The alpha appeals to "the fantasy of being taken care of," writes a reader named Beth. "They allow the woman to stop making decisions, to be taken care of," another reader points out. Readers repeatedly described the appeal of the alpha hero as being the way he tends to the comfort of the heroine.

Chances are, the women reading these books are wives, mothers, and professionals. She is taking care of parents, kids, partners, and colleagues; juggling work, dry cleaning, soccer practice, getting dinner on the table; and planning a date night and finding a babysitter. She's been making decisions all freaking day. (For example, women make 85 percent

of purchasing decisions[4] and that's just one segment.) No
wonder, when this super woman finally gets to sit down, put
her feet up, and relax into a story, she wants to read about a
man who asks her out, plans the dates, calls when he says he
will, and makes the first move. There is a definite appeal to a
man who just takes care of everything for the heroine, right
down to her orgasms, as bestselling and beloved romance
novelist Lisa Kleypas famously pointed out.[5]

For the few hours that she is reading a romance with a
filthy rich alpha hero, a woman is swept into a world where
she is free from her day-to-day responsibilities and having to
think of everything and figuring it all out on her own. She
doesn't have to initiate sex with a guy glued to the TV
because the alpha seduces *her*. She doesn't have to solve
every problem on her own, because the alpha steps up to lend
a hand. The alpha, when done right, is a true partner who
helps her shoulder the burdens, but let's her be who she is.

Romancing the patriarchy

Another interpretation of romance novels with alpha heroes is
that they are the patriarchy versus feminism writ small. The
hero is the embodiment of the patriarchy and the heroine is
the embodiment of feminism and these two must figure out
how to bring out the best in each other and find common
ground in order to live happily ever after.

He will be big and strong, in control of everything, with a
low opinion of a woman's abilities, and he'll "discount the
opinions and emotions of females" in the words of one reader.
She will have to stand up to that, page after page, until he
finally sees her, not as nothing or even as an adversary but as
a partner. Speaking of the romances of the 1970s and 1980s,
bestselling contemporary author Susan Elizabeth Phillips says

"The heroes in these books had all the money, all the power — the heroines none. Yet what happened? She always won. Her courage, brains, and determination trumped the poor hero's macho brawn every time."[6]

This is not unlike a woman's real life: Generations of women grew up being told *a lady does not* or *girls can't*. Only the past few generations of girls grew up being told they could do and be whatever they wanted—but that doesn't mean the world is set up to accommodate that. Numerous studies document how women still face double standards, particularly in the workplace or with regard to her level of sexual experience. A man is seen as a boss, while a woman is seen as bossy. A man is a player, a woman is a slut.

But in a romance novel, oh, the heroine doesn't just make him see her point...she makes him believe in her as a person and she does this without changing herself to be more like a man. She must become a stronger version of herself to start affecting a change. "It starts off with the female being really subjugated and because she has emotional control over the situation, she becomes the powerful one and the one that is given love and is given happiness in the directive," Maddie Caldwell, the romance book club organizer, explains.

It's the battle of the sexes played out between one man and one woman. And in the end, they both win by adopting traits from the other.

A strong hero allows for a strong heroine

Chloe no longer had any fears of being controlled and Chase no longer held back to make sure he didn't push her too far. All that remained was the sweet ecstasy of trust.
And pure love.

—*The Look of Love* by Bella Andre

What can be understood as controlling or domineering in one alpha can be interpreted as confident or decisive in another. Readers found alpha heroes appealing because they're "strong and dependable" (as opposed to those guys who never call back).

But a strong hero also allows for a strong heroine. "I enjoy well-done alpha heroes when paired with heroines who won't be steamrolled," one reader writes. And others echoed those sentiments, writing, "I feel like they can easily over-whelm less-confident heroines." The hero has to be "someone who has enough strength to let the heroine still be herself and do her own thing, manage her own problems, but able to back her up when needed," writes another reader Connie. I'm sure it's true in reverse, too.

When writing about heroines, no one liked the doormat. But the downside of being a strong heroine or real life woman is that the bar is set high for prospective partners. Much as romances may serve as an escape, our taste in fiction can give a clue about what is going in the real world. Is it any coincidence that there was a boom in billionaire hero books during the great recession? Hanna Rosin, in her book *The End of Men: And the Rise of Women,* examines how major social shifts are changing the dynamic between men and women—and how often women are getting ahead while men lag behind. As one group of women improve their lot, "they raise the bar for what they want out of marriage...But the men of their class are failing to meet their standards."

If women turn to romance novels for escape—and a vast majority of them do—no wonder they go for stories of strong, dependable men who are great lovers and partners. Who, you know, meet their standards.

Who said an alpha always has to have a penis?

The alpha character does not have to be male. If we remove penises and gender stereotypes and implications, then what does the alpha character stand for?

Cindy Rizzo, an author of lesbian romances, points out that some lesbian romance "mimics" heterosexual gender roles. "You have the more tough character and the softer character," she says. "Even the softer character, who in straight romance is often the woman, ends up incredibly smart and incredibly clever. In the end, she is the one who steers the ship."

Similarly, when speaking on a panel at the popular romance conference in Washington, D.C., Len Barot (known as Radclyffe, when writing lesbian fiction) points out: "In gay romance, you have a hero and heroine but they happen to be of the same sex. What are the archetypes? They like to see warrior types, those who sacrifice themselves for others." They still like to see an alpha hero. Just as it turns out that we all want someone attractive, confident, and ambitious, it may also be true that many of us desire someone who will be a protector, who will put group interests above their personal interests, or who will simply be a more experienced guide in a relationship, whether sexually or emotionally.

This suggests that "alpha-ness" isn't purely a male phenomenon; women can be alpha, too. It all depends on the character and the context of the relationship. We may have just gotten stuck in a rut of assuming that in romance, alpha = penis person because once upon a time Mills & Boon said so.

Many interpretations of alpha heroes often assume that the reader identifies with the heroine and forgets that the reader often is privy to the point of view of the hero as well. Early romance novels were written almost exclusively in the female POV, though it's far more balanced now. In her essay *The Androgynous Reader*, from the collection *Dangerous Men, Adventurous Women*, Laura Kinsale points out that "authors were actually prevented from using the male viewpoint by their publishers, who clearly operate solidly within the idea that the reader always identifies with the heroine."[7]

But what if she doesn't?

In another essay from the same collection, *The Androgynous Writer: Another Point of View*, Linda Barlow writes:

If the heroine's primary role in the myth serves to encourage us to cope with our fears, the hero's is to provide us with the means of facing and accepting the angry, aggressive, sexually charged components of our personality that we have been taught to associate with masculinity. If romances are a space for women to explore all their thoughts, feelings, why wouldn't they draw from all the characters' experiences that are portrayed in the book? [8]

Similarly, Kinsale writes:

I think that, as she identifies with a hero, a woman can become what she takes joy in, can realize the maleness in herself, can experience the sensation of living inside a body suffused with masculine power and grace...can explore anger and ruthlessness and passion and pride and honor and gentleness and vulnerability: yes, ma'am, all those old romantic clichés. In short, she can be a man.[9]

Now just imagine how *that* woman engages with the world after that experience. By having the experience of tapping into anger, feeling physically powerful, and being sexually experienced, a female reader brings a new strength and awareness to her everyday interactions and experiences. She knows what it's like to be angry and to express it, rather than to cry in the bathroom. She learns what it feels like to take charge of a situation, to make the first move, or to have freedom to move around the world safely.

Romance novels, in a large part, are about women discovering their own strength and power. Some do this by identifying with a heroine who is shown the ropes from an alpha character; others do this perhaps by identifying with the alpha character, feeling his feelings, seeing the world from his point of view, and tapping into all those "masculine" qualities women aren't supposed to possess.

———————

KINSALE POINTS OUT that the courtship in a romance isn't just between two characters, but between different facets of the reader. "That is why romance readers are not, and never have been, intimidated by...the 'retrograde, old-fashioned, macho, hard-edged man'—because the alpha male hero is themselves."[10]

Though popular wisdom would have us believe that all romance novels still feature rapey alphHole heroes, that is a massive oversimplification. And yet, the truth is probably even more simple: Women want a true partner. And most guys probably do, too.

TWELVE

BRA BURNERS AND BODICE
RIPPERS

WHY CAN'T WE ALL JUST GET ALONG?

*I don't want to have to earn love by giving up my ability to
make decisions that determine how I live.*
—*When the Duke Returns* by Eloisa James

WHEN CELEBRATED novelist and feminist Chimamanda
Ngozi Adichie gave her famous TED talk, *We Should All Be
Feminists,* she provided an elegant and eloquent description
of feminism. This feminist also mentioned growing up
reading "every single Mills & Boon romance published"
before the age of sixteen.[1]

Another notable feminist and champion of women's
rights, Ayaan Hirsi Ali also mentioned how influential
romances novels were. "Like many other girls in my class, I
continued to read sensational romance novels and trashy
thrillers, even though I knew that doing so was resisting Islam
in the most basic way...A Muslim woman must not feel wild,
or free, or any of the other emotions and longings I felt when
reading those books."[2]

While Adichie went on to say that those Mills & Boons
were hardly feminist, she also mentioned that she struggled to

read "classic femininist texts," which makes me wonder if maybe she got some ideas about equality between the sexes from romance after all.

There is a supposed disparity between romance and feminism. If the feminists were the man haters, the romance readers were the silly women obsessed with being submissive to dominant men. If feminism championed female empowerment, romance novels, which celebrated men who fiercely growl "you're mine" to the heroine and then end with marriage, were about female enslavement.

Both of these stereotypes are just that—stereotypes, particularly focused on the extreme fringes of each ideology. However, comparing some of the popular perceptions of the values of these two groups (whether they're good, bad, or flat-out wrong) shows tensions between them—why feminists have a reputation for man hating and romances have a reputation for keeping a good woman down.

Whether or not romance novels embody and promote feminist values can be considered from a variety of angles— from the relationship between the characters, the sexual acts they engage in, the topic of conversations between characters, and even how the books are produced.

But what's the deal? Are the feminists missing out on the greatest propaganda for the cause? Or are we, the romance readers and writers, seduced by the patriarchy?

Six reasons romance novels can't be feminist

#1 Because blow jobs

"When I was called a feminist, during those days, my first thought was, *but I willingly give blow jobs.*" [3]writes Roxanne

Gay in her outstanding collection of essays, *Bad Feminist.* Blow jobs seem to be the dividing line between feminist and not feminist.

Elle Keck, an editorial assistant at Avon, tells a story about mixed reactions from her classmates in college when she presented romance novels as feminist works. The men were pretty cool with it, but it was the women in the class who expressed the negativity:

I had a quote in it from *Talk Me Down* by Victoria Dahl and I read it in class to illustrate some of my points. And a girl said "I don't think that's feminist." It was talking about how she really wanted to give the guy a blow job and I was talking about how empowering it was that she was talking about her desires. But this girl said "but she's giving him a blow job. How is that empowering for her?"

How on earth did we get to the point that blow job ≠ feminist?

Is it something about the woman on her knees, a classic position of submission? Is it because it's a sexual act that presumably only gives pleasure to the man receiving it?

"I don't understand how blow jobs are not feminist," says Courtney Milan. "That makes no sense to me! Here's the thing: Does the woman *want* to give the blow job? Ooh, yes she does. Does she get off on giving a blow job? Yeah."

It isn't the act that is inherently degrading or empowering, but the circumstances and intention. Is there choice, love, lust, or pleasure? But if some women think that it's antifeminist to please a man with a particular sexual act, then yes, romances would get a reputation for being anti-feminist. But this notion of "right" or "wrong" sexual acts can have the effect of making people feel ashamed of their desires. How is *that* empowering for anyone?

In romances, there are many, *many* instances of heroes

going down on heroines (or heroines on heroines, or heroes on heroes). On a note of personal observation, I have noticed an increase in historical romance novels published in the last few years that show heroines going down on their hero. And the heroines like it.

#2 Because bodice ripping (said the bra burners)

A clarification: The famous bra burning never happened. In a preview story about feminist protests at the 1968 Miss American Pageant, Lindsy Van Gelder, a *New York Post* reporter, wrote, "Lighting a match to a draft card has become a standard gambit of protest groups in recent years, but something new is to go up in flames this Saturday. Would you believe a bra burning?" Because the Atlantic City Fire Department refused to issue a permit "the ceremonial bonfire" never happened. But it was too late. The term stuck. [4]

However, romance novels have indeed been known to show a blatant disregard for women's attire. It's often interpreted as a symbol of his power over her, and his utter disregard for her modesty or autonomy. Nothing, not even whalebone and heavy cloth or her resistance will stop him. But think about it: Is there any greater feeling than taking your bra off?

Shouldn't ripping off one of the most confining undergarments known to human kind be the most liberating thing ever? Shouldn't the bra burners and bodice rippers go hand-in-hand off into the sunset? Besides infuriating stereotypes and a callous disregard for underthings, what is really going on here?

The common critique of many romances, particularly bodice rippers, is that the hero is so dominant and thus the heroine must be so submissive. In *Fifty Shades of Grey* and other books in that category, it was oh-so-clear by literally using the words "dominant" and "submissive" to describe the roles each would play in the relationship. Many people read no further before casting judgment.

To be fair, there are many romance heroes who are too arrogant, too controlling, too in need of a restraining order. Jane Litte, blogger at Dear Author, offers an alternative understanding of those stories or elements:

Even where there are problematic tropes, like glorification of the borderline abusive boyfriend, or as the stories delve into even darker realms, those characters obviously appeal to some particular emotional interest of a reader. And if we're saying that feminism is the right to choose and to be in control of your own body and desires without judgment, then even the most problematic stories are still feminist stories.

A recent *Time* magazine article also describes *Fifty Shades of Grey* as a story of female subjugation. Christian is one of those borderline abusive boyfriends. In contrast, many romance readers would see a different story: one in which a heroine is able to open up an emotionally repressed man.

Instead of bodice ripping being a way of showing a man's domination of a woman, what if it's a symbol of liberation? In tearing asunder restrictive undergarments, the heroine is freed by strictures of society to be her full self. And in the relationships in these books, the heroes are also given the liberty to feel their own emotions.

#3 Because they're focused on men

Because romance novels are predominantly about a man and a woman falling in love, getting married, and living happily ever after, it's easy for a casual outsider to assume that's *all* it's about. Indeed, one non-romance reader described them as "insipid male-focused nonsense that put women down."

It can be easy to assume women devour these books because they're all about the men and getting the richest, hottest, most powerful one to love YOU and only YOU!

But it overlooks, oh, everything else that happens and all the other situations and characters the characters face. While some romance characters seem to exist in a vacuum, many others show their characters engaging with friends and family. A good number also examine friendship between the female characters. (It also overlooks all the gay romances, some of which are indeed all about men and some of which are not about men at all.)

The Bechdel Test, created by cartoonist Alison Bechdel, is a way to identify any gender bias in works of fiction and it poses the following questions:

- Are there at least two female characters, who talk to each other about something other than a man?
- Do the women have names?

This test is an easy way to determine if a work of fiction is "all about men." Or a man. Most films fail the Bechdel test. A study by the Geena Davis Institute on Gender and Media showed that only 31 percent of named characters were female and only 23 percent had a female protagonist or coprotagonist.[5]

But how do romance novels fare? I would say every romance has a heroine with a name, and in most, every other female character has a name (with the possible exception of some male/male romances, which does not signal misogyny in the same way that, say, an action movie with the only female being the "hot girlfriend" does).

The female characters in romances also have conversations and ones that are not about a man. Of the last four romance novels I read, (including a paranormal, two historical, and a contemporary, not all recently published), three of them included female characters with names talking to each other about something other than a man. The one that didn't was a male/male romance, though it did feature a female character with a name who spoke to the heroes about things other than men or relationships.

Another way in which romance novels are not, in fact, all about the men are the ways in which they are, in fact, all about the women and focus on things that matter to women, like personal acceptance or balancing work, love, and family. When asked to name feminist heroines, many survey responders identified the ones that work or had some sort of occupation, such as Courtney Milan's historical heroines or Julie James' contemporary, high-powered professional women, and that didn't give it all up at the end.

If women want to see a portrayal of women as more than men-obsessed creatures, they might want to pick up a romance novel.

#4 Because damsels in distress

On the tumblr Women Against Feminism, women photograph themselves with a handwritten note saying why they don't need feminism. This is in response to the incredibly popular tumblr Why I Need Feminism, which features photos of people holding handwritten notes saying why they do need feminism. Many of the Women Against Feminism posts want you to know that they are not victims of gender discrimination at all. Nor are they objectified. They don't want "special treatment based on gender," and they can take responsibility for their actions, thanks.

Similarly, many romance novels are slammed because the hero "rescues" the heroine from some god-awful situation, probably involving poverty, pregnancy, kidnapping, highway robbery, being tied up somewhere, sexual dissatisfaction, etc., etc. It's hard out there for a heroine three-quarters into a romance novel.

But the heroine also has some saving of her own to do. There are many instances of kick-ass women physically saving the day. But what we often see is that the heroine saves the hero from a life in a vast, emotional wasteland where not even the slightest feeling can survive.

Women are "the ones that are supposed to be emotionally fluent and men are supposed to be like 'feelings, what, I have feelings?'" says Smart Bitches blogger Sarah Wendell. But she points out that this stereotype is incredibly detrimental not just to the women trying to have a relationship, but also to men. "Emotional fluency is healthy and normal," she says. "And this whole thing about boys not supposed to have emotion is bullshit."

The heroine not only makes him experience all the feelings, but through the constancy of her love, respect, and attraction for him, she also shows that a man can have said feelings without compromising his masculinity or giving up his maleness. This is appealing to women and one reason for the growing popularity of male/male romances written and read by heterosexual women. "It's incredibly powerful for women to see two men doing all the emotional lifting in a relationship with no female there to be emotionally fluent," says Wendell.

Feminism is the social, political, and economic equality

of the sexes. I motion that we include sexual and emotional equality in that, too.

#5 Because they got married and lived happily ever after. With babies.

Does anything reinforce the patriarchal status quo than glorifying marriage with babies as the ultimate in a woman's happiness? After a few hundred pages of a heroine venturing out, traveling the world, sexploring her desires, having conversations with females with names not about men, she ends up right back where she started: in the home, in the nursery.

While there is much to say on the happy ending and how it's not the Worst Thing Ever, let's take a moment to talk about happiness.

We talk so much about how women feel guilty for being too sexy or not being sexy enough, for staying at home or for going to work, for not sticking to her diet or missing a workout, for checking email during soccer practice, or even for indulging a "guilty pleasure" when reading a romance novel.

But romance novels tend to focus less on guilt and more on happiness, and that is a really nice antidote to the pressures we can feel as we rush through the day. "My feminism is that I have the right to be happy," says bestselling author Megan Mulry, who writes smart and sexy contemporary romances with powerful professional women as well as erotic historicals. In a culture always telling us what we should and ought to do to make everyone else happy, the idea of pleasing your own damn self can be pretty revolutionary.

"The female's happiness is the most important part," says Maddie Caldwell. "They're always books by women, for women, about women being happy. That is so fucking good.

What I need is a woman writing a book where a woman is happy and she gets what she wants and that is feminism. Hell yes."

When a woman reads a romance novel, she is choosing happiness. She is choosing her own pleasure. She is choosing to take care of herself. She is declaring that her pleasure is equal to anyone else's.

#6 The ultimate feminist industry?

In conversations about how feminist romance novels may or may not be, so many people I spoke with pointed not to the contents of the books but to the whole business of romance. What started as a few women scribbling stories in their drawing rooms has blossomed into a billion-dollar industry through which many women have found financial and/or personal empowerment.

"I think the business of romance writing is very feminist," Jane Litte of Dear Author says. After all, it is dominated by women—the authors, the editors, the publicists—who are finding success and happiness not by denying their femininity but by reveling in it. Kensington editor Esi Sogah explains just why romance is special: "I think the romance industry is feminist in terms of the ability it gives mainly women to run businesses, earn incomes, express themselves, explore all these things women were told not to think about too deeply."

IN MY SURVEY of romance readers, I asked if one identified as feminist believed in equality but wouldn't use the term feminist, or not at all. Sixty-one percent of respondents replied in the affirmative to the first option. While many commenters expressed their ire at the believe-in-equality-but-wouldn't-use-the-term-feminist option, 35 percent selected this. Just 3 percent said not at all ("The third option makes me cry," one self-declared feminist wrote).

The more I read from both sides, the more I realized that we're more alike than we let on. Whether you call it chivalry or manners, we all want someone to hold the door open for us. We don't want someone else to determine our self-worth —whether that someone else is a man, The Man, feminists, or whomever/whatever. No one wants to be a victim.

We all want equality.

THIRTEEN

THE COVERS

HOLD ME, KISS ME, THRILL ME, CLINCH ME

Clinch, n: *an embrace*

EVERYONE AGREES that if there is one thing that contributes to the bad reputation of romance, it is those god-awful tawdry covers with the hulking shirtless man and the bosomy woman who can't keep her dress on. And the unicorn/stallion/coyote/castle in the background. Everyone is probably wrong.

The truth is, the romance genre had a bad reputation long before Fabio was born and long before there were even covers on books. As early as 1717, romance was considered "a dirty word."[1] And in the romantic period, cheap, mass-produced novels didn't even come with covers. These books "normally reached the public in paper wrappers stitched with thread or temporarily bound in cardboard covered with blue or grey sugar paper," writes William St Clair in *The Reading Nation in the Romantic Period.* Nope, no Fabio. Nope, no books to be sold or judged by their covers. "The first thing most buyers in the romantic period did, before they even took a new book home, was to place an order to have it rebound in leather." Still no Fabio.

The early Harlequins weren't much fancier—they all had unattractive brown bindings. "And the ladies used to ask in the shops for the books with the brown bindings or 'the books in brown.'"[2]

The common wisdom regarding the creation and perpetuation of the clinch cover (that I have heard repeated but wasn't able to verify) depicting an attractive couple locked in a heated embrace is that they were designed to appeal to the merchandise buyers for stores. These were mostly men, presumably ones who liked boobs. One blogger writes, "At that time print runs were determined by preorders from sales reps who bought by the cover. The sales reps were men. It turned out they ordered more books when the covers had busty women, the bustier the better."[3]

Thus it may or may not be surprising that one of the master illustrators behind the covers of many historical romances today is a man. Jon Paul originally turned down an offer to do romance covers because "I saw myself as a fine artist." But he was eventually persuaded by the work of Pino Daeni, one of the greatest romance illustrators. "I was blown away by how beautiful it was." Rather than seeing these covers as tawdry illustrations, Jon Paul sees them as close to classical art.

For all that readers love to hate on the classic clinch cover, they must have some secret fondness for them, because these covers sell—and not just to account representatives who have a fondness for bosoms. There are other types of romance covers available to readers now—some with just a female in a dress or couples on a beach, or there are the "real estate" covers featuring a grand house shrouded in mist. "I think this is one of the things where the mass in mass market comes into play," says Esi Sogah, an editor who has worked at both Kensington and Avon. "I will hear a lot of individual complaints about the beefcake shots. But in terms of numbers, you'll see more [of those covers on] books, clearly signifying that they're selling."

But as much as we roll our eyes ("Ugh, Fabio!") at these covers that "all look the same," there have been changes over the past few decades. A shift in the poses of the couple reflects the changing portrayals of the relationships in the stories, from ones with dominant heroes to ones with more egalitarian relationships.

The bodice-ripping cover

It is the covers of the early romances (yes, the bodice rippers) that many picture as the quintessential romance cover. Perhaps the most wonderfully outrageous example of these is Johanna Lindsay's *Savage Thunder* featuring...Fabio! The couple is in the desert. A black stallion bucks in the background. A mesa rises phallically in the distance. The heroine is on her knees before the hero, seemingly begging, a classic pose of submission. Her pink shirt is falling off. Her red hair (read: feisty heroine!) is cascading down her back as she tilts her head to look up at him. She clutches his fringed leather vest. (Or is she stroking his nipple? Hard to tell.) He embraces her as best he can, while standing in a fairly awkward position. Fabio wears jeans with boots that resemble Uggs. A weapon hangs off his belt. His hair blows in the wind; hers does not.

Gentle Rogue is another Johanna Lindsey title with a classic romance cover featuring...Fabio! This is ship captain Fabio, standing firm on a ship's deck, hanging onto some rope with one hand and the girl with the other. This time he wears black leather pants and a white shirt that is unbuttoned and opened to reveal his broad, muscular chest. The heroine's dress barely hangs onto her body, the sleeves are off the shoulder, there is a slit up to her lady parts and her breasts look ready to burst out of the gown. Interestingly, the heroine of this novel spends the majority of the novel disguised as a boy with her breasts bound. But the pose... She has her back to him, but Fabio seems to be thrusting her against him, holding her tight. Waves crash all around them.

I'm sold. I want this book. This cover promises extreme passion. It's not shy or coy. *It is not ashamed.* As one romance reader commented: "I think the clinch cover is great: It says, in quite unapologetic terms, 'Yes, I am a romance. Within my covers you're going to read about a woman and a man falling in love. Plus, they are going to have sex.'"

For all that sex sells (especially if it's a woman's body on display), a designer for Berkeley Publishing once told me, "Anything hot and sexy usually does well as long as it's taste-fully done and not over the top. Anything too revealing won't be picked up by some of the more conservative buyers so there is a limit to what you can show on the cover without offending some people."

There is also the matter of how the reader feels. She might actually like those beefcake covers but not like the judgment she perceives when she reads them in public. Publishers were aware of this. Jon Paul, the cover illustrator, explains that "in order to solve this problem, they [the publishers] were going to do the step back. They would put a still life with flowers on the front cover, and when you open it up..." there's the clinch we know and love, but only for our private pleasure.

One man. One woman.

The step back was one solution to making readers feel more comfortable about reading a romance in public. Another option was to keep those beautiful illustrations, but portray an individual rather than a couple.

The 1990s marked the era of the lone male on the romance cover. One male in particular. "In the nineties it was driven by Fabio, to be honest," Sogah says. "Bare-chested Fabio was on nearly every cover and if you didn't have Fabio, you got a close substitute." Jon Paul agrees that there was definitely an era where the male dominated romance covers.

But some aspects of men did not dominate. When it came to chest hair and facial hair, Jon Paul, who is hired by publishing companies to create the cover art, says, "whoever is making the decisions is saying they don't want it." That's especially interesting in light of the descriptions of the heroes, many of whom are hardly the waxed, buffed, and polished metrosexual males that are illustrated. Many, many romance heroes have chest hair and facial scruff. Not that you'd know it by looking at the covers.

Another interesting trend in romance covers was the headless hero, in which the cover showcased the man's hot body but didn't interfere with how the reader pictured the hero. You can credit or blame the publisher for these, but "I never do a piece of artwork with a cut-off head," Jon Paul declares.

These days "you don't really see a single man on the cover," he says. "Now it's a single woman. The publishers go through periods."

Especially in historicals, the lone female with the big dress is having a moment. But fun fact: You'll never find those gorgeous dresses available in stores or for rent. "A lot of people compliment me on the dresses," Jon Paul says. "They're totally made up out of my head."

Frequently, the single woman on the cover is not quite alone. In the past decade, her gown might be open in the back (which she obviously didn't do herself), she might clutch a bed sheet, or she might blow a kiss...all suggesting a lover just offstage. However, I have noticed a new, recent trend in covers that portrays just a woman, fully clothed, with a smile to the viewer. One example is Tessa Dare's *Romancing the Duke,* which shows a woman in a striking red gown, smiling and making eye contact with the viewer, all while standing in front of the castle she has just inherited.[4]

Covers like these represent how much the genre is unabashedly female, and how vitally important the heroine's transformation is, on her own and not in relation to a man.

But how well does she sell?

"Regardless of genre you will see at different times, just having a woman on a cover doesn't work as well," Sogah says. "In paranormals in particular we would see that. Even if a series was about an ass-kicking heroine. Those overall didn't sell as well as the ones with a half-naked guy. There were certainly exceptions—but they were exceptions."

Are women—*gasp!*—objectifying men?

According to Jane Litte, the answer is not really. While she does see a growing online trend of objectification of men by woman, the appeal of the hot, buff and naked man cover is the signal it sends to readers. "The male chest cover gives a coded message to the readers," she says. It's "less about the sexual content and more that this is a romance. The more explicit covers are code to romance readers that these are romance books. You're not going to find the naked man on any other type of book."

The updated clinch

In spite of the trends featuring lone men and lone women, the clinch has endured, though the gender dynamics the pose suggests have changed. Covers like the ones on *Savage Thunder* or *Gentle Rogue* project an image of a relationship that is hierarchical, as opposed to a partnership, even though this generally is no longer idealized in popular culture. But the stories have changed. The covers have, too, but not obviously enough to make an impression on the casual passerby.

The clinch cover can, in the words of one reader, "generate a typical dominant male/subordinate female feeling." In reference to the poses on the older covers, I'd agree. However, the way the couple embraces has changed. The man no longer holds the female in a way that suggests his dominance or her captivity. The woman is no longer on her knees; she's either clasping the hero, too, or is on top of him.

A prime example is the cover for *Pleasure for Pleasure* by bestselling author Eloisa James. Both the man and the woman are topless, and the angle of the shot reveals both her back and his six-pack abs. His hands are placed on her waist, and her arm reaches up to hold him. They are equally naked (or "objectified" if you want to be prude and snarky), and their hold on each other mutual.

Or consider the covers for some of my own novels: It's a hero on his knees on the cover of *The Wicked Wallflower,* and the woman is on top of the man on *Wallflower Gone Wild.* For *What a Wallflower Wants* the couple is dancing.

These modern covers are done in the same painted/illustrated style as earlier covers. The layouts are largely the same, often with the author's name featuring prominently. It's easy to see how a slightly different pose has gone unnoticed.

Shades of grey

The latest trend in romance covers was popularized *by Fifty Shades of Grey* and has been repeated endlessly on similar books, such as the *Crossfire* series by Sylvia Day or Maya Banks' novels, which feature fruit or butterflies (next: the birds and the bees?) on black backgrounds. There is no couple and there is almost no color.

These books buck the previous trends in romance, and this may have contributed to their phenomenal success. Because the covers don't scream ROMANCE with all of its implications, more women might have felt comfortable picking them up, reading them in public, or leaving them lying around the house (at least until the world figured out what those books were about).

The popularization of this style of dark, stark cover also coincides with the rise in e-reading devices, which, for the first few generations, only showed the cover illustrations in black and white and as very tiny thumbnail images. The simpler the better happens to be a great visual fit for the content within. For other subgenres, there has been a rise in black and white covers, whether they feature a couple or an object.

This style of cover is also much easier (and less expensive) to create than the classic historical clinch cover, which can be cost prohibitive for an individual to produce. Jon Paul points out the costs of hiring models and renting costumes. There is also location, lighting, and the photographer to account for. "The publisher puts out 1,200, 1,300, 1,400 dollars," he says. That's before Jon Paul gets to work creating an illustration from the photographs. It's done digitally these days, because publishers can no longer wait for oil paint to dry. A lot of people "don't realize what goes into this," he says. It's all beyond the budget of many self-publishers. Having said that, some indie authors and publishers still stage their own photo shoots to create this style of cover because of what it signals to the reader: This is like books you also like.

Many attribute the rise of e-readers to the embarrassment with the usual romance cover. With the cover hidden, no one needs to know what she's reading. It's interesting, then, that many of the covers of books published especially for those e-readers still rely on the classic clinch to signal their readers. Despite the protests, there are still a lot of hot naked man chests.

It's not Fabio's fault

Covers are not the sole source of the bad reputation of romance, though they may not have helped the genre be taken seriously. Many are judged not on the quality of the artistry, but on the fact that they are designed to appeal to women. Jon Paul says, "I remember art directors when I was young said to me 'remember this is women readers.'" Not only are these images for women, but they're incredibly sexy images, glorifying (or objectifying) brawny men. It reminds us all that— gasp!—women like sex. Or it reminds us that women are proud to stand on a cover alone, not needing to reveal any skin, and confidently smile at the viewer. Traditionally, confidence and sexual agency were not qualities our culture liked to see in a woman.

Perhaps it's not that the covers give the books a bad reputation, but that the feminine content of the books gives the covers a bad reputation. "If you go back long enough, before we had such a thing as covers for books, people were still making fun of books written by women about female concerns," says bestselling author Courtney Milan. "I think it doesn't matter what the content is. I think it doesn't matter what the covers are."

The modern version of *Savage Thunder* shows a house in a field with mountains in the distance. The updated version of *Gentle Rogue,* which takes place largely at sea, depicts a London townhouse. But a recently published historical romance by Sarah MacLean features a single woman proudly wearing...breeches! The title, appropriately enough, is *Never Judge a Lady by Her Cover.*

ROMANCE NOVEL HEROINES

What do you think are the most important qualities in a heroine?

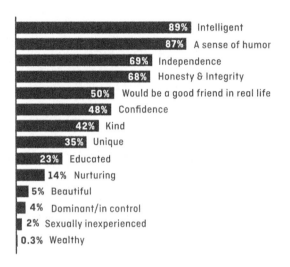

- **89%** Intelligent
- **87%** A sense of humor
- **69%** Independence
- **68%** Honesty & Integrity
- **50%** Would be a good friend in real life
- **48%** Confidence
- **42%** Kind
- **35%** Unique
- **23%** Educated
- **14%** Nurturing
- **5%** Beautiful
- **4%** Dominant/in control
- **2%** Sexually inexperienced
- **0.3%** Wealthy

What readers said about romance heroines:

REAL| I like a STRONG heroine.
(Sometimes strength is found in the unlikeliest places.)
SOMEONE I can RELATE to.|COMPASSION
GOOD SENSE| Willing to TAKE CHARGE of her life.
Doesn't wilt in difficult situations!
Doesn't need a man to save her.|NOT A DOORMAT
GEEKINESS! I love scientists and writers as heroines.
I like the variety of qualities that can be found in the genre.

70% don't care about the age of the heroine

53% think they make great role models

ONLY 1% think heroines should be virgins

77% says it depends on the story

Source: The Dangerous Books For Girls study

FOURTEEN

FROM LEAN IN TO BEND OVER

WHY FIFTY SHADES OF GREY AND LEAN IN
ARE SO POPULAR AT THE SAME TIME

TWO OF THE bestselling books in the past few years were *Lean In: Women, Work, and the Will to Lead* by Sheryl Sandberg (2013) and *Fifty Shades of Grey* by E. L. James (2011). One is a self-help book focusing on how women are held back in the workforce and how to get ahead and become a successful executive, written by a self-made female billionaire. The other is romantic fan fiction about an innocent young girl navigating a dominant/submissive BDSM relationship with an arrogant, controlling billionaire. It was self-published by E. L. James, who made 95 million dollars in its first year of publication, launching her to the top of the list of highest-paid authors. It seems these two books couldn't give more conflicting messages to women: One says to sit at the table, the other says to lift your skirt and bend over it.

What is going on that American women will send these two books to the top of the bestseller lists and keep them there at the same time? A *Newsweek* article finds it "intriguing that huge numbers of women are eagerly consuming myriad and disparate fantasies of submission at a moment when women are ascendant in the workplace."[1] Are there two distinct readerships or are these books together addressing the needs of the modern American woman?

Lean In has sold about 2 million copies—and that is a huge number of books to move in today's publishing environment. *Fifty Shades of Grey* has, to date, sold about 100 million copies. What are these two incredibly successful stories telling us about what women in America want?

Does she want to be the boss or to be bossed around?

The exhaustion of the modern female

Sheryl Sandberg, arguably the heroine of *Lean In*, is exceptional: She's incredibly smart, well educated, and accomplished and balances a marriage and family with her job as COO of Facebook. Her story is one of an intrepid young woman succeeding through intelligence, hard work, and risk-taking.

I'm a huge fangirl of Sheryl, but when I read about her days—up with kids, off to run a major corporation, home in time for dinner with the family, and then back online for a few more hours of email—I am exhausted. I can only imagine how exhausted she must be, as well as all the millions of women like her who are balancing families, careers, and households. These days, 40 percent of families with children under the age of eighteen include mothers who are the sole or primary provider. Of this group, 37 percent have a husband who pitches in and 63 percent are single mothers. Both groups of breadwinner mothers have been increasing over the past few decades.[2]

In the summer of 2012, Anne-Marie Slaughter sparked a massive cultural conversation with her *Atlantic* piece "Why Women Still Can't Have It All."[3] She pointed out that "the women who have managed to be both mothers and top professionals are superhuman, rich, or self-employed." But that doesn't mean the rest of us aren't doggedly pursuing the myth or feeling enormous pressure to succeed at everything, all of the time.

We live in the age of girl power—when we regularly ask women how they manage to have a bikini body two months after the baby, a corner office, 2.5 kids, and date nights with their husbands. This is what American women are supposed to achieve, or at least aspire to. And many do a pretty damn good job or at least put in a herculean effort. You'd think that all these kick-ass women would want to spend their free time (ha, free time!) reading about kick-ass heroines who do manage to have it all. For a few hours, perhaps she could see how it's done, learn what it feels like, and take notes for tomorrow. There are probably many of these heroines as well as readers who adore them.

And then there is Anastasia Steele, a mousey college student in possession of her virginity and in want of a laptop. She somehow captures the attentions of Christian Grey, a young, hot, control freak, and they embark on a relationship exploring roles where he is the dominant who controls everything from buying her underwear to taking it off. He has a chef, a driver, and a whole host of help who ensure that Anastasia never *needs* to do housework. She gets a job; when she has problems with her boss, he buys the company and tries to make her CEO. It is hardly the reality for so many women trying to lean in. But that's exactly the point. Instead of signaling the demise of feminism, the popularity of a character like Anastasia might be a sign that it's succeeding.

In the *Newsweek* article "Working Women's Fantasies," the author writes, "There is something exhausting about the relentless responsibility of a contemporary woman's life, about the pressure of economic participation, about all that strength and independence and desire and going out into the world. It may be that, for some, the more theatrical fantasies of sexual surrender offer a release, a vacation, an escape from the dreariness and hard work of equality."

Elyse Discher, a reviewer for Smart Bitches, Trashy Books, agrees. "I have a crazy, stressful, busy job," she says. "When I come home at the end of the night, my brain is shut down. For me the fantasy of being in a position where you can rely on someone else to take care of everything and know that your needs are going to be met and you're going to be satisfied is appealing."

Romance readers read for entertainment, escape, and relaxation. After staring at a computer screen all day, how nice it must be to imagine being a heroine who doesn't even own a laptop. After making decisions all day, from what to wear that will convey strength and femininity but not be too sexy, to what healthy meal to prepare for dinner that will please everyone, all while trying to convey leadership ability while not coming across as bossy, it's easy to see the appeal of a heroine who doesn't have to worry about any of that. The only thing on her to-do list is Christian Grey.

Where is Christian Grey?

Women are well aware that Christian Grey and other heroes like him are fantasy. We know this because we live in the world.

"It's no coincidence that Christian Grey, billionaire, arrived in the midst of a recession that was often referred to as a 'he-cession' because men were losing their jobs, leaving a growing number of women as primary breadwinners," best-selling romance author and advocate for the genre Sarah MacLean tells *The New York Times*.[4] "All this, and women are still doing the lion's share of household work, child rearing, cooking, etc. Essentially, we live in a time when women aren't only feeling responsible for making a home, they're feeling responsible for keeping the house standing."

In her book *The End of Men: And the Rise of Women*, Hanna Rosin, a writer for *The Atlantic* and Slate.com who frequently focuses on women's issues, details how middle-class women are going to college in record numbers, entering the workforce in droves, and focusing more on advancing their careers than maintaining a relationship while the men in their life...don't.

As the economy shifts from one that values brain over brawn, many men, particularly without college degrees, are left out of work as traditional jobs that would have supported a middle-class lifestyle, such as a factory worker, disappear. And sadly, some of these guys are not qualified—or willing to become qualified—for the new jobs emerging.

"Probably no one has had their wife move up the ladder as far as I've moved down," one man tells Rosin. His wife's philosophy to setbacks is to "build a bridge and get over it." Moving forward seems to be easier for many of the women in the couples Rosin shadows who are doing whatever it takes to advance their careers and support their families than it is for the men who seem more content to get by than get ahead.

One of the main tips Sandberg provides in *Lean In* is to make your partner a true partner. "I don't know of one woman in a leadership position whose life partner is not fully —and I mean fully—supportive of her career. No exceptions." Sandberg encourages women to date all kinds of men, but to marry only someone "who thinks women should be smart, opinionated, and ambitious. Someone who values fairness and expects or even better wants to do his share in the home."

To be fair, men haven't necessarily been set up to succeed at this. "Unfortunately, traditional gender roles are reinforced not just by individuals, but also by employment policies," Sandberg writes. Things like a lack of paternity leave policies make it hard for men to participate at home even if they want to. But it's something that's changing. "Men in younger generations appear more eager to be real partners than men in previous generations."[5]

Until then, it's easy to see how a confident, capable man who carries his own weight is appealing to women balancing some combination of job, kids, and husband. It's even easier to see how it appeals to women who are getting by on their own. For many women today, there just aren't men at the same level of education. "As the women of this second group slowly improve their lot, they raise the bar for what they want out of a marriage...but the men of their class are failing to meet their standards," Rosin writes.

Guess who doesn't lag behind?

"Christian takes control of everything for Ana: finances, career, food, sexual pleasure," author MacLean says. "Anyone who can't see the value in that fantasy is deliberately looking the other way."

Lie back and don't think at all

It is impossible to have a conversation about *Fifty Shades of Grey* without talking about sex.

Beyond the shock and horror that women are interested in sex, especially women of a certain age (that is, not nubile teens, hence the squicky phrases "mommy porn" and "mommy's naughty e-reader"), everyone became shocked and horrified by the kind of sex women were apparently interested in.

Though E. L. James has drawn criticism for her inaccurate portrayal of the BDSM lifestyle, her series did bring the idea of being tied up, spanked, and dominated into the mainstream. Sales of sex toys have skyrocketed.[6] It also made people wonder if feminism had died and if women truly wanted to be bossed around and dominated.

To the contrary, the fantasy of submission can be directly related to having power. "Many people in positions of authority and power are drawn to BDSM, often as subs," write the authors of the book *A Billion Wicked Thoughts: What the Internet Tells Us About Sexual Relationships,* which draws on the unbiased data provided by Internet searches on pornography and romance novels to paint a picture of what turns people on. In fact, when inquiring about the paying members to a website devoted to BDSM, the owner says, "We've got bankers, stockbrokers, Ivy League deans, CEOs. People who have a lot of responsibility in real life, and who want to get away from the burden of being in charge."[7]

It's also interesting to consider this in light of the long history of sex advice for women.

In the Victorian era, proper women were told to "close their eyes and think of England" when they heard their husband's steps outside their door (or so the story goes). This sex was purely for procreation—female consent or pleasure wasn't considered. Talk about being submissive.

But as Western culture became increasingly permissive with regard to having and discussing sex, the advice began to change and the majority of it often focused on how to please a man in bed. For example, in the 1970s, *Cosmopolitan* magazine ran articles on "Things to do with your hands that men like," or "How to turn a man on when he's having problems in bed" and quizzes asking "Are you a good lover?" In 2003, they ran a story "99 Ways to Touch Him: These Fresh,

Frisky Tips Will Thrill Every Inch of Your Guy." The focus wasn't so much on her pleasure, unless it pleased her to get him off. And thus pleasing a man in bed became another skill women had to develop and add to her resume.

Even as magazines began to focus on women's pleasure, the advice was stuff she should do: which sex positions to try (usually the ones that put her in control) or how to masturbate so she knows what to tell her man to do. This modern woman now has to be responsible for the presentation at work, getting the laundry done, and her *own* orgasm, too? Sorry, self, not tonight. I'm exhausted.

In *Fifty Shades of Grey*, Anastasia needs only to lie back and enjoy it. And enjoy it she does. Christian spends more time focused on her experience and her pleasure than anything else. This is largely true of many sex scenes in romance novels that portray countless heroes "lavishing attention" on all parts of the heroine's body. The intense focus on female pleasure is what sets them apart from other portrayals of sex.

Anastasia also doesn't have to worry about touching him the right way or 99 different ways because she's tied up. And what really gets him off is not some acrobatic kinky sex move on her part, but seeing her enjoyment and pleasure. She only needs to lie there and feel beautiful and cherished and know that every damn thing is taken care of, right down to her multiple orgasms. That is the fantasy.

Better together

Instead of being opposed to each other, *Lean In* and *Fifty Shades of Grey* perfectly complement each other. "Sheryl Sandberg speaks to me as my public sphere persona and how I come into my own in the public sphere," explains Maddie

Caldwell, the leader of a romance book club. "And romance novels speak to my personal sphere and how I come into my own as a woman in my own mind."

Somewhere, in the process of trying to have it all or at least holding all their shit together, women don't want to lose themselves. There is a risk of doing just that, of burning out. In a *New York Times* article titled "Madame C.E.O., Get Me Coffee", Sheryl Sandberg and Adam Grant wrote: "In their quest to care for others, women often sacrifice themselves. For every 1,000 people at work, 80 more women than men burn out—in large part because they fail to secure their own oxygen masks before assisting others."[8]

And what do many women do when they're emotionally exhausted? For many, the answer is to read a romance novel. In her book, *Reading the Romance: Women, Patriarchy, and Popular Romance*, Janice Radway reports that "it is the constant impulse and duty to mother others that is responsible for the depletion that apparently sends some women to romantic fiction." There is something relaxing about "identifying with a heroine whose principal accomplishment...is her success...at establishing herself as the object of his concern and the recipient of his care." While I think that is a rather dim and narrow view on all the romance heroines, I think it does fit for Anastasia Steele. She may not be the role model of our day-to-day lives, but that's not her job. She is the fantasy for the exhausted, empowered woman.

"We are never at fifty-fifty at any given moment," Sandberg writes. "Perfect equality is hard to define or sustain—but we allow the pendulum to swing back and forth between us." Likewise, for so many women, the pendulum shifts from *Lean In* during the day to the fantasy of *Fifty Shades of Grey* at night.

FIFTEEN

BECAUSE SHE'S WORTH IT

HOW THE ROMANCE NOVEL HEROINE IS UNLIKE OTHER MASS-MEDIA PORTRAYALS OF WOMEN

MUCH HAS BEEN SAID on the matter of how to be a girl and how to be a woman, from eighteenth century conduct books to glossy magazines today. Much of it has not been said by women. The exception is romance novels.

As much as romance novels are stories of two people overcoming obstacles and falling in love, they're really about the heroine. Her thoughts. Her feelings. Her desires. Her experiences. They are also largely unmediated by men. There are no advertisers requesting editorial changes so the book can better sell deodorant. The female author is writing for a female audience; while there are male authors and readers, the genre isn't trying to appeal to them.

These books are a conversation between women. And a different picture of femininity emerges than from what is traditionally portrayed in other mass media, such as magazines, movies, or television shows. The organization Miss Representation recently researched and discovered that only 29 percent of top speaking roles in Hollywood films are women.[1] Less than a quarter of films feature a female protagonist and even fewer feature leads that are women of color. [2]

In television, women have 43 percent of speaking roles—but they were much younger than their male acting counterparts.[3]

If a woman wants to see a story about a woman—let alone nuanced portrayals of stories about women of different ages, skin colors, social classes, interests, etc.—she'd best stay home, turn off the TV, and pick up a romance novel.

What is especially powerful about the romance heroine is that there are so damn many of them—there is a trope or type for everyone. The genre still has a long way to go in featuring diverse characters in terms of race, culture, gender orientation, or sexual preferences, but it's uniquely positioned to create and popularize different, nuanced, "risky," and interesting portrayals of female characters.

Easy, breezy, beautiful

> *"Look at you. And look at me. We do not belong together."*
> *The thing was, he* had *looked at her and they saw vastly different things. He saw a pretty girl; she saw a plain one.*
> —*The Wicked Wallflower* by Maya Rodale

One way that romance novels succeed in their varied portrayals of women is by allowing them to be complicated in a world that adores the Cool Girl. This archetype is best described by Amy Dunne, the main character in Gillian Flynn's massive bestseller, *Gone Girl*:

> Men always say that as the defining compliment, don't they? She's a cool girl. Being the Cool Girl means I am a hot, brilliant, funny woman who adores football, poker, dirty jokes, and burping, who plays video games, drinks cheap beer, loves threesomes and anal sex, and jams hot

dogs and hamburgers into her mouth like she's hosting the
world's biggest culinary gang bang while somehow maintaining a size 2, because Cool Girls are above all hot. Hot
and understanding. Cool Girls never get angry; they only
smile in a chagrined, loving manner and let their men do
whatever they want. Go ahead, shit on me, I don't mind,
I'm the Cool Girl. [4]

It should be noted that Amy goes fucking crazy after
trying to maintain the charade of Cool Girl, which entails
subverting her own interests and desires to please a guy. In
contrast, in *Bridget Jones's Diary*, Mark Darcy famously
declares, "I like you very much. Just as you are." Which is to
say not a cool girl at all. The journey in a romance is often a
heroine learning *not* to be the cool girl. It is a journey of self-
acceptance, determining her likes and dislikes, vocalizing
them, and finding someone who is okay with her, just as
she is.

The romance novel heroine is allowed to be something
other than "easy and breezy" or "the Cool Girl" or "the hot
girlfriend." But what does the genre have to say on female
beauty?

It is fair to point out that romance heroines are held to
unrealistic standards of perfection, especially in the Old
Skool romances. For example: elegantly arched eyebrows
created without tweezers; a waist so narrow the hero can
wrap his hands around it; long, thick wavy hair that is never
frizzy; violet eyes before the invention of contact lenses;
and occasionally the friendship of talking woodland
creatures.

But the genre has also seen the massive of success of the
delightfully "imperfect" heroine who is not "conventionally"
pretty or a size 2. Some examples might be *Good in Bed* by

Jennifer Weiner, *Bridget Jones's Diary* by Helen Fielding, or *Romancing Mr. Bridgerton* by Julia Quinn.

While survey respondents didn't rank beauty as a very important quality in a heroine—only 6 percent said they preferred heroines to be beautiful—it does matter what the authors say about it.

In the documentary *Love Between the Covers*, bestselling author Beverly Jenkins notes that African American romance was the first time many black women were told they were beautiful. Mass media tends to have a very narrow portrayal of beauty, and it can leave many women feeling like they don't measure up.

If beauty doesn't matter to romance readers, what does? Intelligence. Ninety percent of respondents said a heroine should be intelligent—more than kindness (42 percent), and far more than beauty (6 percent). We're more interested in how a heroine thinks.

"They don't have to be educated but they have to be smart," says reader Rita. Indeed, many readers agreed that it was more important that a heroine be intelligent than be educated (23 percent rated this as important). This could be a nod toward accuracy in historical romance, when most women didn't have many opportunities (or any) for higher education and there were only so many enlightened male relatives who thought a woman should have a proper education (and almost all of them are found in romance novels). It could also be a nod to the diversity of character experiences that romance readers like to see—we may want to read about smart people, but we don't necessarily want every character to be a college student or have a PhD.

While mass media can give the impression that women care only about finding a signature scent or deciphering what his text means, most women want a little more. Many readers wrote about their preferences for heroines that *do something*, other than wait around for the hero to show up and seduce her. "I also like heroines who are good at something, whether they are just smart or whether they are talented in some fashion," says Kim, a reader. Another reader surveyed said she loved to read about heroines with a specific talent, like "writing, art, music, athletics, detective work, etc." Some are more specific: "Geekiness! I love scientists and writers as heroines," says a reader named Samantha.

It almost doesn't even matter what the interest is, so long as it's not just the hero or getting married. "I like to see a heroine who has a strong sense of who she is inside and outside of the relationship," says Julia, a reader. "I want to believe that if something happened to the hero, the heroine would be able to handle herself."

Even if she is not going to be a genius or highly educated or exceptionally talented, she should still be smart. In the reader survey, many wrote in a preference that a romance heroine ought to have common sense and be pragmatic, competent, perceptive, and understanding. Readers wanted to see that she could "think things through before acting" or that she was "someone who can think on her feet." Another added "someone who does not put herself in dangerous or ridiculous situations for the sake of plot points."

Above all, she should not be afflicted with a condition known as Too Stupid to Live (TSTL), which is defined by the blog Heroes and Heartbreakers as "the unfortunate sort of hero or heroine who repeatedly makes irrational, inexplicable, and just plain dangerous decisions that invariably land them in trouble—a technique often used by substandard writers to create conflict or a romantic rescue situation."

What do all these things have in common? They speak to a desire to read about heroines who have interests other than guys and getting married (making them multidimensional and like real women), which is notable considering that one of the main feminist critiques of the romance genre is that the books celebrate and encourage the pursuit of a man and happiness isn't attained until the heroine has his ring on her finger and his baby in her belly. Readers also want their heroines to care about much more than their looks, which is remarkable in light of so many women's magazines and TV shows that emphasize a woman's appearance. If she's going to play the role of Cool Girl, it will only be for a few chapters before she ditches it to redefine Cool Girl as one who feels good in her own skin.

This is not to say there aren't a ton of conventionally beautiful heroines out there and readers that enjoy reading about them (we deal with frizzy hair and such enough in real life, thanks). But these readers' preferences and the genre that delivers them in spades stands in stark contrast to a culture that puts such an emphasis on women's looks that we discuss the attire and hairstyle of women running for president.

Take care

> It isn't a weakness to accept kindness. It isn't a weakness to allow yourself to be cared for.
> —*What I Did for a Duke* by Julie Anne Long

Take care of whom? It is accepted wisdom that women are the nurturing ones in most relationships. We make sure everyone is fed, have clean clothes, go to sleep on clean sheets, etc, etc. We're the ones you cry to, the ones you turn to when you skin your knee or have a hard day at work. We are ever mindful of egos, feelings, and socks on the floor.

When women are encouraged to "take care" of themselves, it so often has to do with tending to their physical selves: manicures, pedicures, highlights, facials. But these serve a deep emotional need and are one of the few socially acceptable ways for a woman to pause from caring for others to have someone care for her. Even if it's just caring for her cuticles.

In romance novels, a woman is able to experience heroes who nurture heroines long and hard and late into the night. Sometimes it can cross the line to "forced comfort" (such as every time Christian Grey commands Anastasia to eat) but often it's a rake who knows how to give her that totally orgasmic experience, the billionaire hero who whisks her away on a private jet for an impromptu vacation, or the hero who plans a picnic.

Sometimes the nurturing can be less glamorous but even more profound. In the historical romance *Captured* by Beverly Jenkins, a mixed-race hero falls in love with a slave. When she is with him, he takes care of her. When she returns to captivity for the sake of her children, he wonders how she fares. "It was a given that no one had brought her breakfast, or drawn her a bath, or shown her how much she was loved."

Interestingly, "nurturing" as a quality possessed by the heroines barely ranked with the readers who took my survey (14 percent said it mattered), reinforcing the idea that these books are as much an escape for women as they can be a reflection of their experiences. One reader wrote, "Doormat heroines who sacrifice themselves for family really annoy me." After a long day of taking care of others, when a woman reads a romance novel, she is nurturing herself—especially if it features a hero who takes care of her. In a world where women are expected to care for everyone else, romance novels are the place where *she* gets taken care of.

Give us five minutes...we'll make you pretty powerful

> *"I had to do something," she said. "I couldn't just sit and*
> *wait for life to happen to me any longer."*
> —*To Sir Phillip, With Love* by Julia Quinn

A heroine should not be a doormat. Reader after reader wrote this when asked what they most disliked about heroines. For one thing, it's boring to read about any character who lacks agency. Similarly, the doormat character is not one who inspires or delivers hope, which is what many people read romances for. Of course, there are beautiful stories of not-strong heroines discovering a backbone—Marissa in J. R. Ward's *Lover Revealed* comes to mind as a perfect example of this type of story.

On the flip side are the beloved and laudable "strong female characters." These can be interpreted as portrayals of women as superheroines out to save the world or fight wars (Katniss Everdeen of *The Hunger Games* or Beatrice Prior of the *Divergent* series), which can feel unrealistic, unattainable, or just plain exhausting to readers who are looking for a relaxing escape. "Too much emphasis has been put on 'kick-ass' heroines," writes Chrissy, a reader. "Excuse me—many women are 'kick ass' because they manage to feed their kids, keep their houses relatively clean, and don't drink themselves into a stupor while doing so."

When most readers wrote about strong heroines, however, it was a different kind of strength than a warrior woman. "I don't necessarily need my heroines to be sword-swinging, wholly self-sufficient people—this doesn't ring true with my real-life experience of people as generally social beings," says one reader. "However, I do like it when heroines take some action in creating their lives and situations—like any real human being would."

The taking of action is key. In an article called "We're Losing All Our Strong Female Characters to Trinity Syndrome" by Tasha Robinson, the author, focusing on movies, notes that "strong female characters" is a phrase said sarcastically and is becoming pointless because, while this strong female character may be portrayed as nuanced, she's pointless if she doesn't *do* anything. The Trinity Syndrome (à la *The Matrix*) is defined as "the hugely capable woman who never once becomes as independent, significant, and exciting as she is in her introductory scene."[5]

In a romance novel, the heroine does not become superfluous to the plot. She *is* the plot. She is not introduced and then set aside for a few hundred pages. The story is of her quest, her adventure, her battles to fight. While the genre has really expanded the hero's role in recent years, these books still present female characters with a crucial role without diminishing them at the end. Robinson writes, "For the ordinary dude to be triumphant, the Strong Female Character has to entirely disappear into Subservient Trophy Character mode." We generally don't see this in romance novels, which are all about the union of a couple becoming stronger and more powerful together.

Readers want to see a heroine who has a sense of self and, as a reader named Mara says, "won't get steam-rolled by the hero," that is, won't turn into a Subservient Trophy Character. Readers want to see heroines with "Strength. Resilience, the ability to overcome adversity." When speaking of an author whose heroines she particularly liked, one reader said, "I like how her heroines aren't damsels— they are smart, independent, funny, and wily, but still have normal vulnerabilities." She doesn't have to be perfect. Or flawless. She has to be real, and she has to be able to carry the story herself.

Readers also like to see heroines making choices *for herself*. "I hate push-over heroines, the ones that let their man make all the choices," says one reader. But not all choices—or decisions—are created equal. Choosing to be a doormat or choosing to sublimate her happiness for others can be off-putting, because it often doesn't come from a place of strength or create a strong foundation for a believable happily-ever-after relationship.

It's not just about a strong female character but also about one who can maintain a sense of agency and self in a relation-ship, especially one with a strong hero. One reader points to *Fifty Shades of Grey*: "Ana was a pushover; she didn't like saying no and agreed to whatever Christian wanted because she was scared of losing him or upsetting him." It's hard to believe that will be a strong basis for a lifetime of happiness together and ultimately, readers want to finish a book feeling that the couple is strong enough, individually and together, to weather any future storms that head their way.

It's a refreshing suggestion that, in a genre about two people coming together in a relationship, we want to see heroines who are willing to piss off their hero in that they are *not* willing to "give up their smarts, their independence, their careers, etc." We don't want to see heroines "lose their common sense or values because they fall in lust with the hero." The genre is at its best when a character can be herself and still exist in a satisfying relationship with another person. It's not either/or, but both.

It comes down to valuing a heroine for herself—her mind, her decisions, her agency—and not just as a paper person to push around for the plot. "I like inner strength and resource-fulness. I like heroines who know who they are and won't apologize for it," says Jennifer, a reader. "Who demand a man love them for that, not in spite of it, who realize they deserve and demand the best." And it comes down to lovers and family members who don't expect her to throw herself on the bomb for them—though she very well may *choose* to do so. What readers really want to see is the story of a heroine who values herself (or learns to) and is valued by other characters, such as the hero or her family.

The ideal heroine is somewhere between the cliché damsel in distress and the kick-ass Katniss-type heroine. The strength doesn't come from being flawless or from super-powers—it comes being an active participant in the creation of your own happiness.

Maybe she's born with it

"No one who had ever seen Catherine Moreland in her infancy would have supposed her born to be a heroine." And so Jane Austen begins *Northanger Abbey* by toying with expectations (already established in 1803!) that heroines are creatures that somehow *inherit* their heroine-ness. But Jane Austen knew and romance readers today know that great heroines aren't "born with it"—they are made. One of the most powerful things about the genre is that the heroine—or hero—on page one is not the same at the end of the book. It's the narrative arc, basic character development, and readers want to see it. And yes, the romance novel is about two char-acters falling in love and overcoming obstacles, but romance novels are at their best when showing how love changes and transforms the individuals.

"I didn't tick off confidence because that's not a require-ment when I start a romance novel, but I want to see both the hero and heroine grow in confidence, respect, etc., by the end

—and that's not for a good romance, that's just good writing," says Jenn, in a comment that was echoed by many. Similarly, romance author Hope Tarr writes, "I like to see heroines who grow as a result of the challenges they overcome in the course of the book, e.g., maybe the heroine doesn't start out as all that confident but by the end, she has grown into her role."

Many readers also griped about "Mary Sue" characters, which the blog Heroes and Heartbreakers describe as "a critical term reserved for badly written protagonists who are too perfect—they are simply good at everything, everyone except the Bad Guys who love them, and they have no discernable character flaws. Mary Sues are generally disliked because, since they have no problems of their own, the conflicts they confront tend to be contrived. As well, with no flaws or quirks, many of them are simply not interesting."

Because the heroine doesn't have to be perfect on page one—or at all—doors are opened for authors to showcase a wider variety of characters, with all kinds of foibles. Readers respond to this. "I don't want a 'well-rounded' heroine with all the perfect qualities," says a reader named Misty. What an awesome antidote to the has-it-all woman who is good at relationships, motherhood, marriage, and her career and still finds time to play tennis and volunteer for charity. Another reader, Stephanie, says "she needs to have serious flaws" and "clumsiness is not a flaw." Seriously, this needs to be acknowledged. There is an entire sub-sub-genre of heroines who don't have complete control over their limbs (I'm guilty of writing one).

An "imperfect" heroine allows for the possibility of transformation—and vice versa. Readers want to see that on her journey she is "honorable and strong" and "interested in becoming a better version of herself." We want to see her take an active role in her journey. What does she transform to?

She becomes a confident woman, who believes in her own worth and value. She becomes a woman who is loved, cherished, and protected, not just by the hero but by other members of her family and the society they live in. And she is a well-pleasured woman.

It's interesting to note that in romance novels, this transformation often takes place without stuff; it's deeper than what is shown on reality TV makeover specials or quick hair/makeup tutorials in glossy lady mags. Even with ugly duckling stories, we often see that there is as much internal character growth as external tweaks. When the hero falls in love with this type of heroine, it's always because he's finally looked past appearances or reputations to see the real woman. And it's typically after she's learned to love herself. Julia Quinn's classic *Romancing Mr. Bridgerton* describes the perfect moment when the heroine realizes this:

"Isn't it nice," the older lady said, leaning in so that only Penelope could hear her words, "to discover that we're not exactly what we thought we were?"

And then she walked away, leaving Penelope wondering if maybe she wasn't quite what she'd thought she was.

Maybe—just maybe—she was something a little bit more.

The idea that a woman can grow stronger through her experiences, and that page-one heroine is not the-end heroine is a powerful one. *This* suggests to women who are unhappy or unsatisfied that 1) things needn't be that way and 2) they have the power to change that.

Maddie Caldwell, the romance book group leader, sums up how this works, and why a genre written by women for women is the place to deliver it: "I think that female writers have a very good sense that you are not the circumstance that you are born into. And yes, we want a fantasy for you. We

want to elevate you in our books. We all want to achieve a
higher position."

Avon: the company for women

There were 158 movies released in 2013.[6] There were over
9,ooo romance novels published in 2013 (and that number
may actually be higher, given that not all self-published
manuscripts have ISBNs to make them trackable). That
means there were over 9,000 romance heroines. It's absurd to
think all of them will appeal to all readers or will include all
the favored traits of a particular reader.

Romance novels are certainly cheaper and easier to
produce than a full-length feature film, which is why we have
so many more. The power of romance is that because of its
relative ease to produce (compared to a TV show or feature
film) more people are able to write and publish a greater
variety of characters.

In spite of the existence of publisher tip sheets, writing
classes, and "conventional wisdom," there is no checklist for
how to write a heroine. Each one comes from the head and
heart of a real life woman. The sheer number of heroines,
written by thousands of authors with different interests and
skill levels, means that there will be a wide range of women
represented. The sheer volume of representations of women
by women is what really sets the romance industry apart from
other media representations.

ROMANCE NOVEL HEROES

What are the most important qualities in a hero?

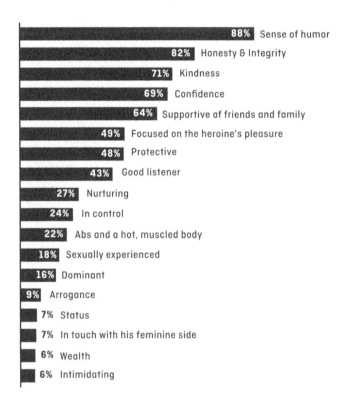

88%	Sense of humor
82%	Honesty & Integrity
71%	Kindness
69%	Confidence
64%	Supportive of friends and family
49%	Focused on the heroine's pleasure
48%	Protective
43%	Good listener
27%	Nurturing
24%	In control
22%	Abs and a hot, muscled body
18%	Sexually experienced
16%	Dominant
9%	Arrogance
7%	Status
7%	In touch with his feminine side
6%	Wealth
6%	Intimidating

Source: The Dangerous Books For Girls study

Do you prefer alpha heroes or beta heroes?

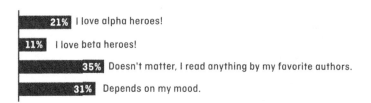

21% I love alpha heroes!

11% I love beta heroes!

35% Doesn't matter, I read anything by my favorite authors.

31% Depends on my mood.

Do romance heroes give real life women unrealistic expectations?

JUST
10%

said yes.

21%

of readers think there aren't enough virgin heroes

ONLY
4.5%

thought heroes should be VERY sexually experienced

70%

say it depends on the story

What readers said about romance heroes:

They need to make the heroine feel like she's **important**.

The sexiest men are the ones with confidence—but he doesn't have to start out that way.

Flawed but a good heart.

Strongly and irrevocably attracted to the heroine—and not afraid to show it.

FANTASY MAN! NOT A JERK.

When a man is very good at what he does it's the ultimate turn-on.

A hot, muscled body does not go unappreciated!

SMART. DETERMINED.

Wild passions barely controlled.

SIXTEEN

REFORMED RAKES AND THE RADICAL NOTION THAT MEN AND WOMEN ARE HUMAN

Oh, God. He was bonding with her. The bonding thing was happening.
—*Lover Eternal* by J. R. Ward

IN THE LAND of historical romance novels, particularly the Regencies, there is no line more quoted than this: Reformed rakes make the best husbands. It's the sort of pithy one-liner a beloved character dashes off and everyone laughs a sparkling laugh, the heroine knits her brow, and the rogue in question scowls but we all know the truth: That bad boy will soon be reformed. And he will like it.

A rake, in this context, is not a type of garden implement but a kind of man. It's old slang for a man prone to all manner of vices, particularly womanizing—and the kind of man your momma warned you about. But his appearance in romance novels is not limited to one historical time period; he's the bad boy, the charmer, the seducer, in any era. Some are shape shifters and vampires; others are small town cops and English dukes. He's a character with endless appeal.

He's slightly different than the alpha male or alphHole in that his sexual prowess is his driving characteristic, rather than the tendency to take charge of everything the way alpha heroes do.

Reform, in this context, means transitioning from a life of freedom, vice, and many women, to a life of loving monogamy and matrimony with one woman.

This type of bad boy and rake is, by his actions and own admission, a horrible candidate for a lifelong monogamous relationship. This is because he loves women, plural. He loves women as creatures to flirt with, do wicked things with, and then leave in the morning. He is a master of seduction, and a woman is typically just another conquest. His relationships with women simply begin and end with sex. There are no tangled heartstrings here. He's got a heart of stone if he has one at all.

Many rakes in the modern historical romance have strict standards: They like their women willing, and they're always focused on her pleasure. The rake tends to avoid virgins, preferring to bed those more experienced in the sensual arts. And high-status virgins are especially to be avoided, since that might as well be an invitation to a wedding or a duel. Funny, since so many male-dominated cultures prize a woman's virginity and "purity." The rake wants none of that.

At first blush, the rake seems like the classic Darwinian male, interested only in sowing his wild oats with as many women as possible and avoiding any commitments of his resources. He would prefer to avoid entanglements like marriage or children—but not at the cost of keeping his pants buttoned up.

The typical reformed rake romance plot is this: Womanizing rogue sets sights on woman and vows to seduce her.

Woman valiantly resists until her passions—stupid, newly awakened passions!—are so inflamed she is begging for the rogue to possess her. To hell with her future, her reputation, anything! The sex happens. It is Oh-My-God Amazing. In fact, it's never been like that before—for either of them. Something has changed: On the way to the bedding, the rake has fallen in love.

And that changes everything.

He has, by previous measures, achieved his conquest. By all rights, he ought to be gone before dawn, but now he wants nothing more than to stay for breakfast and *talk* to her.

Now one night is no longer enough.

And one woman *is* enough.

He was the kind of guy that made a woman want to rip his shirt open and watch the buttons scatter along with her inhibitions.

—*Bared to You* by Sylvia Day

IN 1995 THE book *All the Rules: Time-Tested Secrets for Capturing the Heart of Mr. Right,*[1] a self-help dating guide for women, became a cultural phenomenon by promoting such rules for marriage-minded woman as "don't accept a date for Saturday if he asks after Wednesday" and "always end phone calls first." I was recently perusing the updated version, *Not Your Mother's Rules,*[2] (for, ahem, research) expecting to be revolted by the assumption implicit in the book that all women want to be married and would resort to nefarious tricks to get a ring on their finger.

What I found instead was a call for women to value themselves, or at least act as if they are valuable. Late-night bootie calls are to be declined not because women should be chaste but because if a woman wants more than a man's fleeting, horny attentions, she has to hold out for more than a man's fleeting, horny attentions. (The authors are clear to note that a woman *not* interested in marriage should feel free to enjoy all the bootie calls she wants.). The implicit message is that if you want to be cherished by another person, you have to value yourself as a person worthy of love, respect, and commitment first.

When it comes to playing by the rules in the reformed rake romance, it all falls on the woman's shoulders to set boundaries and enforce them. The successful conclusion of the story hinges on a woman's resistance and determination to avoid sex. All too often real life women are expected to live by this script: Just say no. No means no. We are to avoid dimly lit terraces or dark alleys or frat houses or any other places where we might be compromised. We must watch our drinks. We are to cover ourselves up so as not to tempt men or to be seen as "asking for it." Don't call him first. Because dangerous beasts with appetites for lady flesh roam the earth and we are constantly in danger from being ravished.

Hence the appeal of stories that take a dangerous man and make him safe—which is often how reformed rake stories are interpreted. There is something powerful about the role women play in these stories. She is the lion tamer. She is the one who takes a wild beast and gets him to sit, stay, and come when called. He becomes domesticated enough to sleep in her bed. In a world that gives her so very little power, where a woman's safety is most likely to be compromised by the men in her life, a woman has this. One reader notes these stories can be "incredibly ego-boosting if you're feeling powerless at the time in real life."

But that interpretation doesn't completely capture the dynamic happening here. It assumes that one must be dominant and one must be subordinate. It assumes that one wants monogamy and the other wants all of the sex. It assumes the one who is wild must be tamed.

But this heroine, this woman, is always bundled up and saying no even though—true fact, newsflash, fetch the smelling salts—she might not always want to. She might want to break the rules. She might want passionate nights of wild abandon and multiple orgasms. She might want to benefit from the rake's sexual experience—just imagine how well he knows how to please a woman in bed by now! This heroine doesn't want to tame the bad boy so much as ride off into the sunset with him.

This flies in the face of how we've understood sexual dynamics between men and women. "Most Darwinian models of human origins incorporate females only as passive objects of male competition," wrote biological anthropologists Craig Stanford and John Allen. [3] But that interpretation is changing. "Certainly since at least the mid-90s, evolutionary biologists have known that the dichotomy of 'indiscriminate males' and 'choosey females' was a gross oversimplification," says Dr. Kimberly Russell, an associate professor at Princeton, who holds a PhD in Ecology and Evolutionary Biology, in an interview with *Psychology Today*.[4]

The bad-boy-rake "gives women more permission to let out the inner kick-ass chick," says a reader named Kathryn. And she probably needs it, given how our culture's long-held assumptions about women's lack of sexual interests aren't true and have probably led many women to stifle their true desire. There are consequences, Dr. Russell points out:

If you have a culture that convinces women that 1) they

are less interested in sex (than men) and 2) they are more interested in monogamy, then you create a situation whereby women learn to ignore or disregard their own physical arousal, particularly in situations that are deemed inappropriate.

Romance novels play with this tension between what we're supposed to want and how we actually feel. "Everyone wishes they could cut loose from the social contract every once in a while...and hey, guess what! The bad boy does," says a reader named Jess. And the heroine goes along for the ride, breaking all the rules. One reader points out that the real appeal isn't reforming the bad boy, but "being with a rake or a bad boy" frees the heroine from strictures of society. Seeing the wild side of life sounds like an attractive prospect if you've been living your life by the rules. And let's face it, most heroines do exactly that.

And so do most real-life women, for that matter.

But to get there, she has to make him see that she is not just another conquest, not another one-night stand. She has to believe that she deserves more than that—and must hold out for it. A reader Catherine points out "It's a mark of a heroine's specialness to find a man who responds to her like he does to no one else in the world." It is also a mark of her desirability. Because the rake cannot rely on his usual bag of physical tricks to get this heroine in bed, he has to appeal to more than her body—he has to get to know her thoughts and opinions and see her as a whole human.

And to do *that* she has to believe that her worth is derived from her whole self, not just her sexy parts. She has to believe that she is worth love, worth time, worth attention, and worth the chase. She has to show him what he is missing.

I no longer believed in the idea of soul mates, or love at first sight. But I was beginning to believe that a very few times in your life, if you were lucky, you might meet someone who was exactly right for you. Not because he was perfect, or because you were, but because your combined flaws were arranged in a way that allowed two separate beings to hinge together.

—*Blue-Eyed Devil* by Lisa Kleypas

SO WE HAVE the stereotypical wham-bam-thank-you-ma'am man waking up to discover he has feelings. And we have a woman waking up to the sexual pleasure she has probably been resisting for too long. They have cast off the traditional notions of what they should be like.

And then they live happily ever after (okay, maybe after a few more obstacles and black moments). Because the happy ending is often marriage, it further reinforces the interpretation that these stories are just about making men and women fit into some mold—men are tamed into monogamy and women end up buying right back into the patriarchal system where they pony up a dowry and give up their name.

But what if the real happily-ever-after isn't about the institution of marriage, but about finding that person you can be your whole self with? The reformed rake is "allowed" to become more than the emotionless sex-obsessed creature that old notions of evolutionary biology told us and that traditional ideas of masculinity reinforced. Likewise, the ever-resisting coy female can finally indulge the passionate feelings she's been keeping under wrap. Rather than taming or trapping each other, the reformed rake plot is one of liberation.

If that happens, of course you'd try to stay with that

person forever, not because you need a ring or a vow or want to reinforce traditional gender roles but because it makes you happy. Women can stop resisting, if it feels right. Men can stop chasing, if it feels right. And they can just be. Together.

SEVENTEEN

THE TRUTH ABOUT HISTORICAL ACCURACY

THE SUBVERSIVE WORK OF HISTORICAL FICTION

TO MY EVERLASTING SHAME, I once said that romance novels did not need to be historically accurate. I was a newbie author on a panel at a romance conference and I shared my earnest belief that readers were here for the love story and sexy times; they were not here for my hot take on the Corn Laws. As long as no one rolled up to a Regency ball in an automobile, all was good. It might not be totally wrong, but it is not right and definitely not the full picture.

In Romancelandia, historical accuracy is highly prized, but its definition is subject to fierce debate. Readers will write outraged letters to authors critiquing their history when that author actually has a PhD in history. My fellow authors and I would joke about writing in fear of "The Regency Police" which was our term for the sort of reader who will slam an author in reviews for writing "wallpaper historicals" or getting small details about corsets and carriages wrong, which therefore ruined *the entire book* for them.

This is not an essay about innovations in carriage design

or when whalebone went out of fashion. To be clear, when I am talking about historical accuracy in this essay, I'm interested in big picture representation, the thoughts and yearnings of characters, and their behavior. It matters, because historical accuracy can be used as a tool of patriarchal oppression and white supremacy, but it can also break us free from all that.

What I have come to understand is that what we claim to be "historically accurate" is a statement about value and who matters. It has profound implications for the stories we choose to read, write and celebrate. It especially matters with our popular fiction because this is where, for better or for worse, many people learn about history.

When discussing the romance genre, it is also impossible to understand what we mean by "historical accuracy" without also understanding what we mean by "escape".

Everything I needed to know about history I learned from historical romance

In Janice Radway's infamous book, *Reading the Romance: Women, Patriarchy and Popular Literature*, she interviews a group of romance readers she calls The Smithton Women about their romance reading habits and preferences. One theme that emerges repeatedly is the idea of romance as an escape, usually from a woman's daily cares and worries. But another frequently and strongly cited reason for reading romance is "to learn about faraway times and places." In other words: education.

Radway understands this as a justification for reading romance, because a person (usually a woman) is spending time on herself for her own pleasure rather than in service to the needs of her family and/or employer. This is apparently a terrible thing for a woman to do and so there must be a good reason for her to do so (which is such a troubling sentiment). Being able to say "well it's educational, it's about history" goes a long way to shutting down snark from people you can't ignore, like members of your own family.

In the case of The Smithton Women, they were reading Harlequins and the classic 1970's bodice rippers. Whether these representations of "faraway times and places" and the characters who inhabit them are accurate, honest, or appropriately sensitive is an important conversation to have. Another important conversation to have is which authors are best positioned to write those types of stories. (I will not be doing a deep dive into those texts here). Even historical fiction readers I meet today tell me one primary reason they read the genre is to learn about history. What I want to focus on with this essay is the fact that *people turn to popular historical romance and historical fiction to learn about their own history*.

The Smithton Women mention learning about faraway times and places, but by the nature of the book, it is history told from a woman's point of a view.

The type of history we get from historical romance and popular historical fiction is the kind I think many of us hunger for—the one about people who look like us, with experiences that are relevant to ours. It is the history that does not center on the accomplishments of white men, or a token queen, but talks about the lives, drama, accomplishments and relationships of everyone else. Because historical fiction is written in a way to be easy and engaging to read, the dynamics between people come alive, leap off the page, and make the history effortless to learn and understand. The history in fiction isn't a list of facts, it is a world we become immersed in as we read. It is often the history of women or other marginalized groups—the "hidden histories" to use a popular marketing term.

It is also the history that is deliberately not taught in schools. This is by design.

In her book *Mothers of Massive Resistance: White Women and the Politics of White Supremacy*[1], Elizabeth Gillespie McRae describes a deliberate effort made by white women in the early half of the 20th century to maintain segregation in society in ways that did not run afoul of federal law. They had a variety of techniques, but most involved taking over school boards, summer camps and essay contests to promote "racial distance." They especially got involved in what was being taught in schools; one particular strategy they employed with textbook content was to ensure that Black people were only ever portrayed as anonymous laborers, if they were even mentioned at all.

Gillespie McRae writes:

"There was almost complete erasure of black history and black Americans from Mississippi's textbooks. This erasure certainly had damaging effects on black students, but they had their families, their churches, and their schools to tell them stories that challenged such hegemony. White south-erners raised on a segregated history and living in a segregated society only had stories that upheld a natural order of white over black."

If Black history is missing from the curriculum, it's not an accidental oversight. To a lesser extent, women's history is largely absent from most curriculum as well, save for the celebrations of a few token women in women's history month. One thing we lose with this erasure is a sense of power, pride, accomplishment and respect. Black people were never just laborers; they were poets, activists, scientists, inventors, bankers, teachers. Women were never just wives and mothers; they went to school, earned a living, banded together to change the world's expectations for what women could accomplish. What we lose from this erasure is enormous: a common understanding of our history and humanity.

This effort to whitewash history and erase the accomplishments of women and other marginalized groups isn't all in the past, either. Recently, the state of Texas recently fought to pass a law[2] that no longer requires schools to teach "historical documents related to the civil accomplishments of marginalized populations including women's suffrage and equal rights, the civil rights movement, the Chicano movement, the American labor movement and Native American rights." To cut the women's suffrage movement—in which women of varying backgrounds and classes banded together for a sustained and non-violent revolution to enfranchise half the population—is to cut out some of the most effective political organizing in history. It is no wonder that a story of female solidarity overthrowing the social order is not to today's youth.

In short: the history taught in schools is a way to engineer the present. Trying to erase a legacy of accomplishment, activism or even mere *existence* is a way to diminish real people today.

Enter historical fiction. Thus far, it is not within the purview of any school board (though too many groups are banning books in libraries). Publishers are making bank with "hidden histories" that celebrate precisely these stories. We are all The Smithton Women, who want not just an escape, but an opportunity to learn.

"But it's just a novel!" one might cry in frustration. It is not *just* a romance novel. It is an alternative point of view of history. It is vividly portrayed characters, often based on or inspired by real people. It's not just their work and accomplishments but their full lives. Suddenly, we, the readers, have a new understanding of ourselves in the context of history and of each other and it becomes increasingly difficult to maintain or enforce a sense of inferiority, invisibility or distance with each other.

The "Regency"

The Regency Era in England lasted for just nine years, from 1811 to 1820. It is also the setting for approximately ten million romance novels. The Regency as many historical romance readers know it, is one created by Georgette Heyer in the 1930s. Yes, she was drawing on the works of Jane Austen and to an extent, we are all rewriting *Pride and Prejudice* explicitly or implicitly. Yes, there is a long, rich tradition of "silly novels by silly novelists" between Austen and us. But we can thank Heyer for the froth, the banter, the high society hijinks that many of us associate with a Regency romance.

We have been copying her ever since. The Romance reader/writer cycle goes something like this: reader reads romance novels. Love! Reader writes romance novel of their own, the kind they like to read. Perhaps this reader/writer is keen to publish their work and so they focus more on what sells, which is what they like to read, so they write more like that and so on and so forth until infinity.

Partly out of love, partly out of the practicalities of publishing, we reinforce this notion of Regency until it feels like gospel true fact and readers write angry reviews when anything strays from it. Even if it is actual fact.

It applies to race. It also applies to our understanding of

"propriety" and "sexy times" and use of the word *fuck*. It applies to expectations for a certain type of heroine, a certain type of hero. It applies to the idea that a happy ever after (HEA) must have marriage and babies or someone needs their money back.

However. Book by book, some authors are pushing at the boundaries, loosening the corset if you will. Maybe the hero doesn't rape his wife, even though it was perfectly legal to do so (until 1993 in America, by the way). Maybe the heroine is a proper lady but she also learns to read and likes to—gasp— read novels and no one beats her for it. Maybe there was sex that was fun and raunchy and not at all for procreation. Maybe someone said the *f* word (in use since the 16th century). Maybe the story centers around a hero/hero or heroine/heroine because gay people have always existed and fallen in love. Maybe the hero and heroine do not get married, but they still live happily ever after together.

We can expand the genre book by book. Because this is the other part of the romance reader/writer cycle: reader loves romance but can't find exactly the book they want, reader decides to write it themselves, reader gets it published and discover they are not the only one who wished for that exact story.

The Regency is a fun era because there were so many rules of social interaction and courtship to flaunt—or observe. Imagine knowing just what the rules were for every social interaction, for fashions that were slow to change and were mostly flattering for every body shape, for knowing all you had to do in life was get married and have a (male) baby and all the challenges and hard stuff of the world would just be handled by your husband who wouldn't beat or rape you even if it was his legal right to do so. Imagine worrying only about menus someone else will cook, and not at all worrying about racism or feminism or being woke. I can see how a reader today might wish for that escape.

But a young lady would never!

One of the most heartbreaking questions I get as an author is "how do you write a historical heroine with agency?" In other words, how do you write a historically accurate, but dynamic female character? To me, this question reveals a perception of historical women as passive, constrained creatures who lived small, uninteresting lives. Similarly, one of the most common critiques I get as an author is that my heroines are "too modern." Modern is never defined. But both lead me to the same question: do we really think that women were doormat wives and mothers for ten thousand years, having tea parties and doing laundry, until one day, say in 1973, when they got the right to reproductive autonomy and credit cards and could wear pants?

Women today are the heiresses of radical historical women who did not accept the constraints society placed on them. They are legion.

Once you go looking for them, these "modern" radical rule-breaking women are everywhere in history. Deep in my research on the Gilded Age and women's suffrage movement in the second half of the 19th century, I noticed something: the same female names kept popping up in each other's biographies. Women were running fashion houses and mail order businesses and establishing franchises (Madame Demorest). They were publishing newspapers (Mrs. Frank Leslie) and writing for them (Nellie Bly, Ida B. Wells, Winnifred Black, Fanny Fern, Jane Cunningham Croly, Lillie Devereaux Blake). They were inventing the dishwasher (Josephine Cochrane, with my eternal gratitude), becoming doctors (Dr.

Elizabeth Blackwell, Dr. Rebecca Lee Crumpler, Dr. Mary Putnam Jacobi), establishing settlement houses (Lillian Wald, Jane Addams, Victoria Earle Matthews), and engaged in political organizing (Susan B. Anthony, Elizabeth Cady Stanton, Matilda Joslyn Gage, Mary Church Terrell and literally *thousands* more).

Women were working in factories, in department stores, on the streets. They were organizing. In 1909, a young woman named Clara Lemlich led a strike of twenty thousand female garment workers; they all flooded the streets of New York until they got better wages, shorter hours and safer working conditions. For all the talk about "a woman's sphere" it sounded like she wasn't at home much. She was out in the world, getting shit done.

I can't speak for everyone, but I don't remember learning much "women's history" in school. One time, after my World History class (which focused exclusively on Europe and the French Revolution), I stayed after class to ask my teacher about the women. He suggested that I read about Germaine de Staël. But that was all he had to offer to a girl who wanted to know more about her history.

So I have turned to biographies in addition to historical fiction. One evening, while lamenting the lack of biographies on certain women, my husband pointed out a lack of subjects. I told him that wasn't true. He pointed out a lack of source material. This can be true, though is not always true. To study, say, Nellie Bly, who basically invented investigative journalism in America and burst open the newsroom doors for women to follow, it might take more hunting through archives scattered around the country than doing yet another "Founding Father" biography where all the source material is neatly collected and preserved. And annoyingly, there is only one, out-of-print biography about Nellie Bly. In my experience, it is often the case that there is only one, out-of-print biography of a particular historical woman. Alas! But it is enough to prove that somewhere, at some time a young lady most certainly did do whatever is claimed she wouldn't or couldn't. It is enough to spark the imagination of a novelist.

Imagine if the market existed for these biographies! It does, in a way: it's "hidden histories" and historical fiction and historical romance. We can take whatever factual information there is and imagine the rest of it to write compelling stories that keep these women alive.

You find what you are looking for

When I wanted to write a series about Gilded Age heroines in New York City who had a secret club and were all entrepreneurs, I found *plenty* of historical records to support it—there was the Sorosis Society (badly named, but very cool) in the 1870s. Later, there was the Heterodoxy Club based in Greenwich Village, full of radical feminists intent on changing the world. There was the Colony Club, a gorgeous uptown haunt for wealthy women. That is not even half of it. Sometimes that's how it happens: as an author, I get an idea and look to see if the historical record supports it.

But if I had just relied on the history I learned in school or the sense of history I had from film and television, I would have missed it. I would have just one book on Germaine de Staël and two movie versions of *Pride and Prejudice*.

The idea of historical accuracy is a lens through which we do our research. That means the questions we ask, the source material one looks for, the records we examine, the libraries we go to.

When we search for people of color existing all over the world, in all different eras, doing interesting things, we find it. When we search for women who did interesting things, we find it. When we search for Queer history, we find it. People have been people for a long time, openly and joyously themselves, and they left evidence for us. We just need to look for it. We need to decide who is worth searching for. We need to decide who is valuable.

Escape

What we talk about when we talk about historical accuracy is what kind of escape we are looking for, which is really talking about what kind of world we want to live in or how today's world is making us feel. Show me your idea of escape, show me your idea of historical accuracy and I'll have a good idea of your politics. It has taken me a long time to understand that.

I have been perplexed by reviews that declare some historical romances "too modern" or "wallpaper historicals." These were novels in which the heat level was the same, the banter was playful and easily read, everyone went to Almack's and sipped lemonade, the forms of address were correct, no one rolled up to a house party in a car. It was never the spies or the pirates that they complained about, either. *What was so inaccurate?*

To some extent, with historical romance, it is the language. A Grace Burrows novel, with leisurely Austen-esque writing sounds very different than, say, a Julia Quinn novel. But to a greater extent, I think it is the *yearnings* of the characters that can feel modern. Does the heroine desire true love, and is she content to only be a wife and mother? Is the hero out of touch with his emotions but at ease with his power?

And so I have come to understand that there are different

kinds of escape people seek from their romance novels. There are readers who wish for an escape into a historical time where one did not have to worry about feminism or racism or being woke or where the duke's fortune came from. When one did not have to worry about social media, changing fashions, climate change and putting gas in the car. When the hard things were remembering the steps of a quadrille and how to address a duke in a variety of situations. When children could be sent to the nursery upstairs and one could live their adult life in clean clothes laundered by someone else. When a heroine was happy to be submissive because the duke could —and would—take care of her. It was okay that she didn't have any legal rights because her love and relationship was so strong and secure.

And there are those who wish for an escape into a story where a heroine with problems and yearnings similar to ours are resolved into a HEA. We want all that we love about a historical setting, but also a safe space for readers. We do not want to make that groove from Georgette Heyer any deeper.

In conclusion

We can rewrite history with the historical romance novel, so to speak. We can do the job that history textbooks fail at, due to a concerted effort from conservatives who understood the power of who gets to be deemed significant and celebrated, and who gets space on the page. We, the historical novelists and our readers, can bring life and light to the "hidden histories" of which there are so, so many. And with book after book after book, we can demonstrate who is and was worthy of love and value. Reading book after book after book that normalizes a more inclusive history can help normalize a more inclusive present. We can craft stories about people living their best lives, finding love and joy and happy ever after—no matter what historical era they lived in, or how little they were considered at that time. This, I think, is one of the most revolutionary and subversive things the historical romance can do. If we choose to do it.

NOTE: *This essay was added in the 2023 edition and did not appear in the original version of the book.*

EIGHTEEN

HAPPY EVER AFTER

WHAT'S SO FUNNY ABOUT PEACE, LOVE, AND UNDERSTANDING?

ROMANCE NOVELS END HAPPILY. This is what distinguishes the books from other love stories, such as *Romeo and Juliet* or *Gone with the Wind*. While often criticized for glorifying marriage (and thus trapping women in a patriarchal system), the romance novel isn't about wedding bells at all. The happy-ever-after (HEA) is ultimately about the triumph of hope, acceptance, and justice. The happy ending is also what makes romance novels dangerous books for girls.

And they got married and lived happily ever after

"And they got married and lived happily ever after" is a well-worn, hackneyed phrase that ends many a fairy tale. But it's curious: While marriage in real life was seen as the ultimate life goal for much of human history, novels that portray the marriage of the characters as the ultimate resolution get a bad rap for doing so. But as the institution of marriage and the cultural attitudes toward it have changed over time, romance novels have evolved to reflect this while still remaining true to the definition of the genre. Thus we can get a glimpse of what the HEA is really about—and it's not the wedding.

Some detractors believe that HEA = marriage and that a story of female empowerment cannot end with a wedding. Thus, romance novels are terrible for women. "Critics claim that the romance novel extinguishes its own heroine, confining her within a story that ignores the full range of her concerns and abilities and denies her independent goal-orien- tated action outside love and marriage," Pamela Regis writes in *A Natural History of the Romance Novel.* It supposedly "binds readers in their marriages or encourages them to get married; it equates marriage with success and glorifies sexual difference."[1]

But if we see many romance novels ending in marriage, it's because they were set in a world where getting married is what you did, especially if you found true love. Of course, there were economic, social, and religious considerations as well. What marriage is, how it works, who gets to do it, for how long, and how well individuals fare in it is a continually vexing subject (and beyond the scope of this book).

Some have seen marriage as oppressive to women: Her father walks her down the aisle, hands her over like property to the groom. She subsumes her own identity, takes his name, and gets busy keeping house and making babies. For a woman to *choose* marriage—as romance heroines so often do —is interpreted as women voluntarily buying right back into the patriarchal system that oppressed them in the first place. When that uppity, adventurous heroine says "I do" in the end, it supposedly "reaffirms its founding culture's belief that women are valuable not for their unique personal qualities but for their biological sameness and their ability to perform that essential role of maintaining and reconstituting others," writes Regis.

Historical romance novels often portray marriage because this is an accurate reflection of the time in which these novels are set, and probably just as important, because marriage was a pre-requisite for sex. But even historical romances don't always *end* with marriage—in popular tropes like the arranged marriage or marriage of convenience, the story begins with "I do" (however grudgingly it may have been said). The real HEA in these stories is when the characters have fallen in love and declared it. It's not over until everyone says "I love you."

Long before gay marriage became legal in the United States, there were romance novels featuring gay and lesbian couples. While it was a small subgenre at first, it's been growing. In the documentary *Love Between the Covers*, long-time fans of lesbian romance spoke about how powerful it was to read stories about same sex relationships that ended optimistically. Even without a wedding, there could still be an emotionally uplifting conclusion to a love story. Thanks to forward-thinking members of Romance Writers of America, these stories are ensured to be part of the genre.

Those members of Romance Writers of America in charge of finding a short, pithy, all encompassing definition for "romance novel" made sure it was inclusive. "There were those who insisted that the genre prohibit adultery and require marriage at the end, and there were those who pointed out that some people should keep their moral standards out of other people's stories," romance author Jennifer Crusie writes in an excellent blog post on the process. "There were those who suggested that the definition include 'love between a man and a woman.' And there were those who pointed out that it would be a bad idea to make RWA officially homopho-bic, given that respected publishers like Naiad Press have been publishing lesbian romances for years. We'd like this definition to be reflective of the twenty-first century, not the nineteenth."[2]

And it is: The definition is "a love story that has an emotionally and optimistic ending." There is no mention of who is allowed to love, or not. And there is no mention of marriage.

The demographics of marriage have shifted radically since the days of the first romance novels. Now more people have the legal right to marry. People marry at a later age, people live together before the wedding, people live together without having a wedding, and some people get divorced and then do it all over again.

But the HEA carries on.

We now see the rise of the "happy for now" ending instead of happily ever after, particularly in contemporary romance novels, which strive to represent an emotionally optimistic conclusion to a story set in a modern world, read by a reader with modern values. When people don't usually get engaged after a few dates, what does the HEA look like? "I've been seeing it more in contemporaries that they don't necessarily have to be married or engaged at the end as long as there's a resolution to whatever was hindering their relationship from moving forward," says Elyse Discher, the romance reviewer.

A popular new subgenre of contemporary romance, New Adult, focuses on characters of college age. Widely reported statistics show that the younger people marry, the more likely they will end up divorced. Can we have 22-year-olds falling in love and getting married and have modern readers believing they'll make it forever and ever? It might be challenging. It's also beside the point. "They don't need to put a label on it," Discher said, whether that label is man, wife, boyfriend, girlfriend, The One, or whatever. What readers want to see in these stories is that the characters "worked through this major issue," which provides a sense of optimism that these characters will be able "to get through the smaller ones that inevitably follow."

The happy ending of a romance novel is not about marriage at all—it's about hope for a better future.

Dangerous books for girls

If romance novels just reinforced the idea that heterosexual marriage and adhering to traditional gender roles is the key to a lifetime of happiness, they wouldn't be so revolutionary. Or if romance novels ended tragically, they would have been handed out with conduct books and collections of sermons. It is the happy ending, which champions hope, love, and acceptance above all, that make these stories so powerful and revolutionary.

The happy ending, in which the villains are punished and the good are rewarded, is an endorsement of everything that happened in the story. In a romance, Jennifer Crusie writes, "the lovers who risk and struggle for each other and their relationship are rewarded with emotional justice, unconditional love in an emotionally safe world." Is there any better reward than that? It's not about the money, the aristocratic title, the marriage certificate. The romance novel declares, via the happy ending, that love is the most important thing, and that love can exist between people, no matter how they identify or whom they love. And love doesn't care about any rules.

The power of the HEA goes deeper than just a morality tale. It is one that inspires hope and it seductively suggests that you, dear reader, might want to try this at home.

When a woman reads a romance novel, she is declaring

that her needs and desires are valid and should be satisfied. When she reads a romance, she embarks on a journey in which she can identify with the hero, heroine, or any number of characters, giving her a richer understanding of herself. When she reads about faraway lands, other time periods, different types of people, and a variety of experiences, she gains a deeper understanding of the world. This alone is empowering.

"But on that journey, we get this one contract," bestselling contemporary romance author Jennifer Probst points out. That contract between the reader and the writer says, "In the end everything is going to be okay. When we're picking up a romance novel, we're saying you can take me on this rough roller coaster ride, but I'm going to go for it because you're going to make it okay in the end."

Knowing the story will end well means that it's safe to feel more deeply as we read, which intensifies and *personalizes* the reading experiences and makes the story seem so real. When a reader sees and *feels* these characters living, loving, and triumphing in a fictional world that seems remarkably like the one she lives in, it feels possible. Or when the story features fantastical creatures in imaginative worlds that still have remarkably human emotions, it suggests that perhaps this isn't just fantasy. Maybe, just maybe, this dream can be a reality.

The happy ending of a romance novel is an endorsement of female value, female agency, and female pleasure. It also conveys hope that we can make these fantasies into our realities. It is this declaration about the power of an individual woman to transform herself, her relationships, and her world that has made romance novels dangerous books to the status quo, and thus dangerous books for girls.

NINETEEN

WHY IT MATTERS HOW WE TALK
ABOUT ROMANCE NOVELS

*She didn't know why arguing this point had become so
important to her. If he wanted to live out the remainder of
his life bitter and alone, she supposed he had that right. But
his smugness made her so prickly all over. And he wasn't
merely insulting love and romance. He was insulting her
friends and acquaintances. Her own hard work.*

The innermost yearnings of her heart.

*This wasn't an academic argument. It was personal. If
she didn't defend the idea of lasting happiness, how could
she hold out any hope for her own?*

—*Romancing the Duke* by Tessa Dare

THERE IS a sense of shame surrounding the reading of a
romance novel. Eighty-nine percent of romance readers think
people look down on them for the reading material, 52
percent report feeling shame for their reading habit at some
point in time, and 51 percent think they should keep their
reading secret.

"I used to buy romance novels and hide them," says
Courtney Milan, a bestselling author and champion for

romance authors. "I would get books I didn't want to read and I put the romance novels under them when I went to buy stuff."

Almost everyone I spoke with had a variation on the same story of their early romance reading years. "I went to library to get them. I didn't want my dad to know, so I would have my tote bag and get three [other] books on top," says Elle Keck, the editorial assistant. Elyse Discher told me: "I used to bring them to school with me and I would hide them because if someone saw me reading one my life would obviously be over."

And Maddie Caldwell, the reader group leader, told me, "I had all my romances stacked behind my shoes, so my mom wouldn't find them. Yes, I literally kept them in my closet."

Novels form an unfortunately large proportion of the habitual reading of the young at the exact crisis of life when the spirit is at once most susceptible and most tenacious...when the experience affords no criterion whereby to separate the true from the false in the delineations of life...
—"False Morality of Lady Novelists" by William Rathbone Greg (1859)

MOST READERS discover romance novels at the same age, often in the same way: As young girls, they snuck them from their mom's bedside table, grandma's bookshelf, or their sister's closet. They read them illicitly, vaguely aware that these stories are somehow bad or wrong or something to be embarrassed by. Why else would they be tucked away in the closet? Why else wouldn't we talk about reading them?

This, I suspect, is how our culture is able to perpetuate a

stigma against a certain literary genre without ever saying a word. This is how we "just know" that reading romance novels is a shameful act. Because romance novels are so obviously and unabashedly *female*, we're not just communicating snark toward the books, but snark toward women and girls.

Romance novels feature nuanced portrayals of female characters having adventures, making choices, and accepting themselves just as they are. When we say these stories are silly and unrealistic, we are telling young girls not to expect to be the heroines in their own real lives.

Romance novels depict female sexuality as a loving, pleasurable, and above all acceptable part of being a happy woman. But when we call them smutty, dirty, or trashy books, we are negating that message.

Romance novels portray life as we, women, would love it to be. One that recognizes our worth, rewards us for our confidence, and supports our choices. When we say these books are unrealistic, we are telling young girls, who might still be open-minded about their own opportunities, that they should lower their expectations.

Romance novels show a variety of heroines, be they plain, pretty, plump, or skinny. They might be black, white, rich, poor, gay, or straight. But when we say only stupid women read these books, we are telling young girls that they are foolish for believing that they can be beautiful and lovable just the way they are.

Even when we don't talk about romance novels, we are sending a message that women are not worth talking about and that they should be seen and not heard.

We communicate these messages to girls at their most vulnerable age. A majority of my survey respondents, 40 percent, discovered romances between the ages of 11 and 13.

Another 29 percent were between the ages of 14 and 18. This is the age when girls are learning how to be women. This is also the age when girls start losing confidence: "At the age of nine a majority of girls were confident, assertive and felt positive about themselves. But by the time they reached high school fewer than a third felt that way," *The New York Times* said in a report on a major study examining self esteem in adolescence.[1] This is the age when to do something #LikeA-Girl goes from being a badge of honor to an insult.

Because romance novels are by women, about women, for women, what we say about them can be interpreted as a statement on how we value women (or don't). If we care about the messages we send to impressionable young girls—and all women!—then we should care about how we talk about romance novels.

AT THE START of this book, I had the noble goal of defending and redeeming the genre's reputation. I believed it was of vital importance that these books received the critical respect they deserve. But the more I wrote and researched the subject, the more I came to realize that the status of the romance novel is inextricably linked with the status of women in our society. To change the perception of the genre, we would have to change some other deeply ingrained cultural values. I don't think it's a coincidence that as the status of women has increased, so too has the status of romance.

What has made the romance genre so successful is also what has contributed to its bad reputation. Romance novels are, relatively, cheaply made, mass-produced items. They will probably never be perceived to be the same value as something expensively produced in limited quantities. And yet, the widespread availability of these cheap books has meant that entertaining and uplifting literature was readily and affordably available to a greater audience. This is a good thing.

There are things we can do to combat the snark: Put romance in the curriculum in schools, put these books on the same shelf as Literature, and watch what we say about it.

But here's the other thing I have come to realize: We may not want to change the reputation of romance.

It was toward the end of writing and researching this book that I came across this passage from *The True Story of the Novel* by Margaret Anne Doody, which cast everything in a new light:

By making the novel so officially unimportant, so harmless, the definition permitted the Novel to continue, and Novels to be bought. Such a definition even encouraged (if slowly) further writing by women, and the production of novels in which female characters play central roles.[2]

Perhaps the romance genre didn't flourish *in spite of* its bad reputation, perhaps it thrived *because* of it. A lack of reviews meant no one in positions of authority was watching, so Lady Authors were free to write whatever they wanted. A lack of prestige meant that men weren't interested in trying their hand at romance, thus interrupting all those female voices. Jokes about heaving bosoms and throbbing members meant that those who tried to ban or regulate sexual expression didn't focus on this frivolous, euphemistic purple prose. Everyone knew these were stupid, trashy books so we didn't have to worry about them.

Like the "fallen" or "ruined" heroine of many a romance novel, perhaps a bad reputation isn't a death sentence, but a passport to freedom.

While many readers feel that romance has a bad reputation, many don't give a damn. They love the genre and don't care who knows it. Fifty-six percent are "out" as a romance reader and another 37 percent are out with "certain people." You, or someone you know, could be reading romance novels.

If there is one lesson that I have learned from every romance novel I've ever read and every conversation I had for this book, it is this: To hell with what anyone else tells you and follow your heart.

THANK YOU!

Thank you so much for reading *Dangerous Books For Girls*. I hope you enjoyed it. I also hope it makes you feel good about reading romance novels and eager to shout your love from the rooftops.

If you found this book entertaining, interesting, thought-provoking or [insert adjective of your choice here], there are a few things you can do next:

Talk to your friends. True fact: personal recommendations are the #1 way readers find new books. Help a friend (and an author!) by telling your friends about *Dangerous Books For Girls* and starting a conversation about romance novels. You may be surprised to discover secret romance fans among your friends!

Leave a review. This is another way to help get this book into the hands and onto the e-readers of fellow readers. As a reader and an author, I appreciate all reviews, whether raving or scathing.

Subscribe to my newsletter. For more details and to sign up please visit: www.mayarodale.com/newsletter. This is the best way to stay notified about my writing, my events and to access exclusive subscriber benefits.

Read a romance novel! I share many "must read" suggestions on my website:https://www.mayarodale.com/must-reads. You'll also find Mama Rodale's Infamous Romance 101 Syllabus!

Bring *Dangerous Books for Girls* to Book Club. Not that any group of romance readers needs prompting to talk about the genre they love, but I invite you all to read Dangerous Books for Girls and to check out the book club kit on my website at https://www.mayarodale.com/dangerous-books-for-girls. You can also contact me to inquire about my availability to join your book club for a discussion via Zoom.

Cheers to my fellow romance fans and thank you so much for reading!

ACKNOWLEDGMENTS

This book would not be possible without the contributions of so many people and I will be eternally grateful to all of them.

My mother, for making me read romance novels in the first place.

My professors at NYU, particularly Gabrielle Starr, Susan Ostrov Weisser and Stacy Pies for their guidance and encouragement in my studies of women, fiction and romance.

I am especially grateful to the people who generously took an hour or two out of their busy days to talk to me about romance: Bella Andre, Bobbi Dumas, Brenda Chin, Cindy Rizzo, Courtney Milan, Eloisa James, Elle Keck, Elyse Discher, Esi Sogah, Jackie Horne, Jane Litte, Jenn Northington, Jennifer Probst, Jon Paul, Kate McMurray, Madeline Caldwell, Olivia Waite, Petra Mayer, Sarah Frantz Lyons, Sarah Wendell and Tessa Woodward. Special shout out to Megan Mulry for a great interview, beta-reading and encouraging text messages. Special thanks to Lisa Lin, Amy Valentini, Maria Almaguer and Allisia Wysong for sharing their expertise on romance novels with me in our Facebook group.

Major thanks to everyone who participated in the surveys associated with this project. I asked *a lot* of questions and was so grateful to receive a lot of thoughtful responses.

Everyone I surveyed and interviewed had smart, fascinating, insightful things about the genre and shared what romance has meant to them, personally. I feel lucky to have had these conversations. While I wasn't able to include everything everyone said (alas!), each survey response and conversation helped to shape my thinking and was a valuable contribution to this project.

Very special thanks to:

My editor for this project, Madeline Caldwell. You made this book so much better, lady!

My copyeditors, Nancy Bailey and Shelbi Stoneback. Any remaining mistakes are my fault.

My designer, Tokiko Jinta for beautiful work on this book and related materials.

My husband, Tony Haile, my romance hero IRL.

ABOUT THE AUTHOR

 Maya Rodale is the best-selling and award-winning author of funny, feminist historical romance and historical fiction. A champion of the romance genre and its readers, she is also the author of *Dangerous Books For Girls: The Bad Reputation of Romance Novels, Explained.* Maya has reviewed romance for NPR Books and has appeared in Bustle, Glamour, Shondaland, Buzzfeed, The Huffington Post and PBS. She began reading romance novels in college at her mother's insistence and has never been allowed to forget it.

Visit Maya online at www.mayarodale.com.

ROMANCE NOVELS BY MAYA RODALE

The Gilded Age Girls Club

Duchess By Design

Some Like It Scandalous

An Heiress To Remember

Keeping Up With The Cavendishes

Lady Bridget's Diary

Chasing Lady Amelia

Lady Claire Is All That

It's Hard Out Here for a Duke

The Wallflowers

The Wicked Wallflower

Wallflower Gone Wild

What a Wallflower Wants

The Writing Girls

A Groom of One's Own

A Tale of Two Lovers

The Tattooed Duke

Seducing Mr Knightly

Three Schemes and a Scandal

Anthologies

At the Duke's Wedding

At the Christmas Wedding

At the Summer Wedding

NOTES

1. What We Talk About When We Talk About Fabio

1. Raphel, Adrienne. "What Happened to the Harlequin Romance?" *The New Yorker*. May 08, 2014. www.newyorker.com/business/currency/what-happened-to-the-harlequin-romance.
2. *U.S. Book Industry Year-End Review*. Report. February 25, 2014. www.nielsen.com/us/en/insights/reports/2014/u-s-book-industry-year-end-review-2013.html.
3. Milliot, Jim. "Publishing's Holding Pattern: 2014 Salary Survey." PublishersWeekly.com. September 19, 2014. www.publishersweekly.com/pw/by-topic/industry-news/publisher-news/article/64083-publishing-s-holding-pattern-2013-salary-survey.html.

2. The Romance Revolution

1. While all these literary terms have very different definitions and even canons, for the purposes of this book, I'm going to use the term romance novel since it's most widely understood today and the result of all these different literary subgenres devoted to women's interests.
2. "About the Romance Genre." MyRWA: The Romance Genre. www.rwa.org/p/cm/ld/fid=578.
3. Jack, Belinda Elizabeth. *The Woman Reader*. New Haven: Yale University Press, 2012.
4. Rathbone Greg, William. "False Morality of Lady Novelists." In *Victorian Print Media: A Reader*, edited by Andrew King and John Plunkett. Oxford, England: Oxford University Press, 2005; 50–54.
5. S. "What Is the Harm of Novel-Reading?" In *Victorian Print Media: A Reader*, edited by Andrew King and John Plunkett. Oxford, England: Oxford University Press, 2005; 48–49.
6. St Clair, William. *The Reading Nation in the Romantic Period*. Cambridge, U.K.: Cambridge University Press, 2004; 309.
7. St Clair, 309.
8. St Clair, 309.

9. Moss, Gabrielle. "The Rise of the Reactress." Slate.com. www.slate.-com/blogs/browbeat/2015/02/20/sienna_miller_and_the_rise_of_the_reactress_what_her_roles_in_american_sniper.html.

10. Crusie, Jennifer. "Romancing Reality: The Power of Romance Fiction to Reinforce and Re-Vision the Real Romancing Reality: The Power of Romance Fiction to Reinforce and Re-Vision the Real." Accessed March 24, 2015. www.jennycrusie.com/for-writers/essays/romancing-reality-the-power-of-romance-fiction-to-reinforce-and-re-vision-the-real/.

11. St Clair, William. *The Reading Nation in the Romantic Period.* Cambridge, U.K.: Cambridge University Press, 2004.

12. Coontz, Stephanie. *Marriage, a History: From Obedience to Intimacy or How Love Conquered Marriage.* New York: Viking, 2005.

13. Radway, Janice A. *Reading the Romance: Women, Patriarchy, and Popular Literature.* Chapel Hill: University of North Carolina Press, 1984.

14. Edgeworth, Maria. *Belinda.* Oxford, England: Oxford University Press, 2008.

15. Coontz, 180.

16. Salmon, Edward G. "What Girls Read." In *Victorian Print Media: A Reader*, edited by Andrew King and John Plunkett. Oxford, England: Oxford University Press, 2005; 68–72

17. Rathbone Greg, William. "False Morality of Lady Novelists." In *Victorian Print Media: A Reader*, edited by Andrew King and John Plunkett. Oxford, England: Oxford University Press, 2005; 50–54.

18. Chatel, Amanda. "The 6 Most Common Sexual Fantasies for Women Might Surprise You." Bustle. January 2015. Accessed March 24, 2015. www.bustle.com/articles/61918-the-6-most-common-sexual-fantasies-for-women-might-surprise-you.

3. Proof Of Snark

1. Mahler, Jonathan. "Bodice-Ripper in New Hands." *The New York Times*, May 02, 2014. http://www.nytimes.com/2014/05/03/business/media/news-corp-to-acquire-harlequin-enterprises.html?_r=0.

2. Bosman, Julie. "Penguin and Random House Merge, Saying Change Will Come Slowly." *The New York Times.* July 01, 2013. http://www.nytimes.com/2013/07/02/business/media/merger-of-penguin-and-random-house-is-completed.html.

3. Baron, Jesse. "Bad Romance." Harpers Magazine. February 2014. http://harpers.org/archive/2014/02/bad-romance/.

4. Dederer, Claire. "Why Is It So Hard for Women to Write About Sex?" *The Atlantic.* February 19, 2014. http://bit.ly/1fosdZL.

5. "Let's Read About Sex." *The New York Times.* October 05, 2013. www.nytimes.com/2013/10/06/books/review/the-naughty-bits.html?pagewanted=all.

6. MacLean, Sarah. "Letters." *The New York Times.* October 19, 2013. www.nytimes.com/2013/10/20/books/review/letters.html?_r=0.

7. Giraldi, William. "Finally, an Academic Text Devoted to 'Fifty Shades of Grey'" TheNewRepublic.com. May 19, 2014. www.newrepublic.com/article/117814/50-shades-grey-academic-study-feminist-point-view.

8. Luther, Jessica. "Beyond Bodice-Rippers: How Romance Novels Came to Embrace Feminism." TheAtlantic.com. March 18, 2013. http://bit.ly/15mkBhS.

9. Dumas, Bobbi. "Don't Hide Your Harlequins: In Defense of Romance." NPR. December 18, 2013. Accessed March 24, 2015. www.npr.org/2012/12/18/167451651/dont-hide-your-harlequins-in-defense-of-romance.

10. Sachs, Andrea. "The Global Boom in Bodice-Rippers." *Time.* September 21, 2009. Accessed March 24, 2015. www.time.com/time/magazine/article/0,9171,1921627,00.html#ixzz0cOquKNTq.

11. Radway, 28.

12. Shaffer, Andrew. "How Paperbacks Transformed the Way Americans Read." Mental Floss. April 19, 2014. http://mentalfloss.com/article/12247/how-paperbacks-transformed-way-americans-read.

13. Grescoe, Paul. *The Merchants of Venus: Inside Harlequin and the Empire of Romance.* Vancouver: Raincoast Books, 1996.

14. Grescoe, 89.

15. St Clair, 39.

16. *Romance 2012 Books and Consumers US Genre Profile.* Report. August 7, 2013. www.bookconsumer.com/store/product.php?id=85.

17. Ibid.

18. *Ibid.*

19. "Online Retailers Gained, While Brick-and-Mortar Lost in Wake of Borders Exit." Bowker. August 6, 2013. Accessed March 24, 2015. www.bowker.com/en-US/aboutus/press_room/2013/pr_08062013.shtml.

20. "Did You Know?" NoraRoberts.com. http%3A%2F%2Fwww.noraroberts.com%2Fdid-you-know%2F.

21. Weiner, Jennifer. *A Moment of Jen.* February 13, 2015. http://jenniferweiner.blogspot.com/.

22. Weinstein, Adam. "Where Are the Women Writers?" *Mother Jones.* April 4, 2014. Accessed March 24, 2015. www.motherjones.com/me-

dia/2012/04/women-writers-vida-asme.

23. Donahue, Deirdre. "Scholarly Writers Empower." *USA Today.* July 10, 2009. www.usatoday.com/life/books/news/2009-07-06-romance-novels_N.htm.

24. Regis, Pamela. *A Natural History of the Romance Novel.* Philadelphia: University of Pennsylvania Press, 2003.

25. Donahue, Deirdre. "Scholarly Writers Empower." *USA Today.* July 10, 2009. www.usatoday.com/life/books/news/2009-07-06-romance-novels_N.htm.

4. Trashy Books

1. Weissmann, Jordan. "The Decline of the American Book Lover." TheAtlantic.com. January 21, 2014. www.theatlantic.com/business/archive/2014/01/the-decline-of-the-american-book-lover/283222/.

2. St Clair, 178.

3. St Clair, 179.

4. Radway, 21.

5. Mansel, Henry Longueville. "Sensation Novels." In *Victorian Print Media: A Reader*, edited by Andrew King and John Plunkett. Oxford, England: Oxford University Press, 2005; , 55–57.

6. Ballaster, Ros. *Seductive Forms: Women's Amatory Fiction from 1684 to 1740.* Oxford: Clarendon Press, 1992; 36.

7. St Clair, 205.

8. Radway, 23.

9. Grescoe, 3.

10. Poovey, Mary. *Genres of the Credit Economy: Mediating Value in Eighteenth- and Nineteenth-Century Britain.* Chicago: University of Chicago Press, 2008; 305.

11. St Clair, 186.

12. St Clair, 244–245.

13. Radway, 22.

14. Grescoe, 45.

15. Donahue, Dierdre. "Scholarly Writers Empower the Romance Genre." *USA Today*, September 08, 2009. http://content.usatoday.com/community/comments.aspx?id=35564302.story&p=3.

16. St Clair, 201.

17. St Clair, 202.

18. Poovey, 285.

19. Poovey, 157.

5. How Lady Authors Drive Innovation In
Publishing

1. Rathbone Greg, William. "False Morality of Lady Novelists." In *Victorian Print Media: A Reader*, edited by Andrew King and John Plunkett. Oxford, England: Oxford University Press, 2005; 50–54.
2. Rosin, Hanna. *The End of Men: And the Rise of Women.* New York: Riverhead Books, 2012.
3. Howey, Hugh. "July 2014 Author Earnings Report." Author Earnings. July 2014. Accessed March 24, 2015. http://authorearnings.com/report/july-2014-author-earnings-report/.
4. Zacharius, Steven. "Self-Publishing: The Myth and the Reality." The Huffington Post. December 16, 2013. Accessed March 24, 2015. http://www.huffingtonpost.com/steven-zacharius/selfpublishing-the-myth-a_b_4453815.html.
5. Madrigal, Alexis C. "Sorry, Young Man, You're Not the Most Important Demographic in Tech." TheAtlantic.com. June 8, 2012. http://theatln.tc/1xez0k6.

6. For Love And Money

1. Hale, Shannon. "The Nitty Gritty on Authors, Signings, and Filthy Lucre." 'squeetus' January 13, 2015. http://oinks.squeetus.com/2015/01/the-nitty-gritty-on-authors-signings-and-filthy-lucre.html.
2. Eliot, George. "Silly Novels by Lady Novelists." In *Silly Novels by Lady Novelists.* Penguin Great Ideas. London: Penguin UK, 2010.
3. Copeland, Edward. *Women Writing about Money: Women's Fiction in England, 1790-1820.* Cambridge: Cambridge University Press, 1995. P 165
4. *Love Between the Covers.* Directed by Laurie Kahn. Released in 2015.
5. Austen, Jane. *Pride and Prejudice.* New York: Barnes & Noble Classics, 2003; 178.
6. *Pride and Prejudice*, 178

7. Romance Versus Realism

1. S. "What Is the Harm of Novel-Reading?" In *Victorian Print Media: A Reader*, edited by Andrew King and John Plunkett. Oxford, England: Oxford University Press, 2005; 48–49.

2. "Uncanny Valley." Wikipedia. Accessed March 23, 2015. http://en.wikipedia.org/wiki/Uncanny_valley.

3. Talbot, Margaret. "Pixel Perfect—The New Yorker." *The New Yorker.* April 28, 2014. www.newyorker.com/magazine/2014/04/28/pixel-perfect-2.

4. Reeves, Clara. *The Progress of Romance.* New York: The Facsimile Text Society, 1930; 110.

5. Reeves, 111.

6. Doody, Margaret Anne.*The True Story of the Novel.* New Brunswick, NJ: Rutgers University Press, 1996.

7. Oliphant, Margaret. "The Byways of Literature: Reading for the Million." In *Victorian Print Media: A Reader,* edited by Andrew King and John Plunkett. Oxford, England: Oxford University Press, 2005; 196–206.

8. Horne, Jackie C. "Dukes: The 0.0001735%." November 22, 2013. http://romancenovelsforfeminists.blogspot.com/2013/11/dukes-00001735.html.

9. "List of Countries by the Number of US Dollar Billionaires." Wikipedia. Accessed March 24, 2015. http://en.wikipedia.org/wiki/List_of_-countries_by_the_number_of_US_dollar_billionaires.

10. "Google Search Results." Google. Accessed March 24, 2015. www.-google.com/webhp?sourceid=chrome-instant&ion=1&espv=2&ie=UTF-8#q=youngest+billionaire+in+america.

11. Milan, Courtney. "Rake Mathematics: A Deleted Scene." Rake Mathematics: A Deleted Scene | Courtney Milan, Historical Romance Author. http://www.courtneymilan.com/rakemathematics.php.

12. Giraldi, William. "Finally, an Academic Text Devoted to 'Fifty Shades of Grey'" TheNewRepublic.com. May 19, 2014. www.newrepublic.-com/article/117814/50-shades-grey-academic-study-feminist-point-view.

13. Crusie, Jennifer. "Romancing Reality: The Power of Romance Fiction to Reinforce and Re-Vision the Real." Jennifer Crusie. Accessed March 24, 2015. www.jennycrusie.com/for-writers/essays/romancing-reality-the-power-of-romance-fiction-to-reinforce-and-re-vision-the-real/.

8. What We Talk About When We Talk About Bodice Rippers

1. Tetel, Julie. "On the Term 'Bodice Ripper'" Julie Tetel Andresen's Blog: The Anatomy of Language and Love. June 9, 2014. www.-goodreads.com/author_blog_posts/6432127-on-the-term-bodice-ripper.

2. Bly, Mary. "A Fine Romance." *The New York Times.* February 11, 2005. www.nytimes.com/2005/02/12/opinion/12bly.html?_r=0.
3. Joyce, Brenda. *Deadly Caresses.* New York City: St. Martin's Paperbacks, 2007.
4. See the 2015 *Sports Illustrated* swimsuit edition cover.
5. Theilen, Jacqueline M., MD. "Sexual Health. Viagra for Women: Why Doesn't It Exist?" May 8, 2014. Accessed March 24, 2015. www.mayoclinic.org/healthy-living/sexual-health/expert-answers/viagra-for-women/faq-20057960. And Vernon, Polly. "The Race to Discover Viagra for Women." TheGuardian.com. April 24, 2010. www.theguardian.com/society/2010/apr/25/women-viagra-polly-vernon.
6. Doody.
7. Acton, William. *The Functions and Disorders of the Reproductive Organs in Childhood, Youth, Adult Age, and Advanced Life: Considered in Their Physiological, Social, and Moral Relations.* 3rd Edition. London: Churchill, 1862; 101.
8. Rogers, Rosemary. *Sweet Savage Love.* New York: Avon Books, 1974; 228.
9. Crellin, Olivia. "Historic California Rape Law Tells College Campuses: 'Yes Means Yes'" Vice.com. September 29, 2014. http://bit.ly/19MSthI.
10. Goldberg, Eleanor. "As Risk of Female Genital Mutilation More Than Doubles in U.S., Lawmakers Take Action." The Huffington Post. February 6, 2015. Accessed March 24, 2015. www.huffingtonpost.com/2015/02/06/female-genital-mutilation-us_n_6629460.html.

9. Pure Heroine

1. St Clair, 188.
2. Virgin, 147.
3. Virgin, 77.
4. Collins, Gail. *When Everything Changed: The Amazing Journey of American Women from 1960 to the Present.* New York: Little, Brown and, 2009; 169.
5. Turner, Natasha. "10 Things That American Women Could Not Do Before the 1970s." Ms Magazine Blog. May 28, 2013. http://ms-magazine.com/blog/2013/05/28/10-things-that-american-women-could-not-do-before-the-1970s/.
6. Collins, 167.
7. Wendell, Sarah, and Candy Tan. *Beyond Heaving Bosoms: The Smart Bitches' Guide to Romance Novels.* New York: Simon & Schuster, 2009; 25.

10. Lady Porn

1. Wendell, Sarah. "Romance, Arousal, and Condescension." Smart Bitches, Trashy Books. March 15, 2012. http://smartbitchestrashybooks.com/2012/03/romance-arousal-and-condescension/.
2. Orenstein, Peggy. *Cinderella Ate My Daughter: Dispatches from the Front Lines of the New Girlie-girl Culture.* New York, NY: HarperCollins, 2011.
3. "Sin City's Missing Sexual Education." TheDailyShow.com. February 11, 2015. http://thedailyshow.cc.com/videos/67hgfz/sin-city-s-missing-sexual-education.
4. Fisher, Mary Anne, PhD. "How Much Do Romance Novels Reflect Women's Desires?" *Psychology Today.* July 16, 2010. www.psychologytoday.com/blog/loves-evolver/201007/how-much-do-romance-novels-reflect-womens-desires.

11. The Real Appeal Of The Alpha

1. Grescoe, 50.
2. Wendell, 72.
3. Vail, Elizabeth. "The ABCs of Romance: The Duke of Slut, Mary Sue, TSTL, and More!" Heroes and Heartbreakers, January 19, 2012. www.heroesandheartbreakers.com/blogs/2012/01/the-abcs-of-romance-the-duke-of-slut-mary-sue-tstl-and-more.
4. "Marketing to Women: Quick Facts." She-conomy.com. May 07, 2008. http://she-conomy.com/facts-on-women.
5. Wendell, 73.
6. Rodale, Maya. "9 Surprisingly Feminist Romance Novels to Read During 'Read a Romance' Month," Bustle.com. August 8, 2014. www.bustle.com/articles/33655-9-surprisingly-feminist-romance-novels-to-read-during-read-a-romance-month.
7. Kinsale, Laura. "The Androgynous Reader: Point of View in the Romance." In *Dangerous Men & Adventurous Women: Romance Writers on the Appeal of the Romance*, edited by Jayne Ann Krentz. Philadelphia: University of Pennsylvania Press, 1992; 37–54.
8. Barlow, Linda. "The Androgynous Writer: Another Point of View." In *Dangerous Men & Adventurous Women: Romance Writers on the Appeal of the Romance*, edited by Jayne Ann Krentz. Philadelphia: University of Pennsylvania Press, 1992; 55–64.
9. Kinsale, 45.
10. Kinsale, 47.

12. Bra Burners And Bodice Rippers

1. Adichie, Chimamanda Ngozi. *We Should All Be Feminists.* London: Harper Collins, 2014.
2. Ali, Ayaan Hirsi. *Infidel.* New York: Free Press, 2007; 94.
3. Gay, Roxane. *Bad Feminist: Essays.* New York: Harper Perennial, 2014.
4. Collins, 199.
5. Smith, Stacy L., Marc Choueiti, and Katherine Pieper. *An Investigation of Female Characters in Popular Films Across 11 Countries.* Report. September 2014. http://seejane.org/wp-content/uploads/gender-bias-without-borders-full-report.pdf.

13. The Covers

1. Doody, Margaret Anne. *The True Story of the Novel.* New Jersey: Rutgers University Press, 1997; 281.
2. Grescoe, 44.
3. Tetel, Julie. "On the Term Bodice Ripper." Julie Tetel Andresen's Blog: The Anatomy of Language and Love. June 9, 2014. www.goodreads.-com/author_blog_posts/6432127-on-the-term-bodice-ripper.
4. Side note: Those backgrounds are also made up by the artist. Jon Paul tells a funny story of a model coming to a photo shoot with her mother, who expected to see elaborate sets with luxurious couches and dramatic castles. But nope, those are all added later, out of the imagination of Jon Paul.

14. From Lean In To Bend Over

1. Roiphe, Katie. "Working Women's Fantasies." Newsweek.com. April 16, 2012. www.newsweek.com%2Fworking-womens-fantasies-63915.
2. Wang, Wendy, Kim Parker, and Paul Taylor. "Breadwinner Moms." PewSocialTrends.com. May 29, 2013. http://pewrsr.ch/1xv1dDG.
3. Slaughter, Anne-Marie. "Why Women Still Can't Have It All." June 2012. *The Atlantic.* www.theatlantic.com/magazine/archive/2012/07/why-women-still-cant-have-it-all/309020/.
4. Cowles, Gregory. "Inside the List." *The New York Times.* February 21, 2015. www.nytimes.com/2015/02/22/books/review/inside-the-list.html.
5. Sandberg, Sheryl, and Nell Scovell. *Lean In: Women, Work, and the Will to Lead.* New York: Knopf, 2013.

6. Velez, Natasha, Gabrielle Fonrouge, and Natalie O'Neill. *"Fifty Shades of Grey* Whips Sex-Toy Sales into a Frenzy." NewYorkPost.com. February 14, 2014. http://nypost.com/2015/02/14/fifty-shades-of-grey-whips-sex-toy-sales-into-a-frenzy/.

7. Ogas, Ogi, and Sai Gaddam. *A Billion Wicked Thoughts: What the World's Largest Experiment Reveals about Human Desire.* New York: Dutton, 2011.

8. Grant, Adam, and Sheryl Sandberg. "Madam C.E.O., Get Me a Coffee." *The New York Times.* February 07, 2015. www.nytimes.com/2015/02/08/opinion/sunday/sheryl-sandberg-and-adam-grant-on-women-doing-office-housework.html?_r=0.

15. Because She's Worth It

1. "Media Literacy with a Gender Lens." TheRepresentationProject.org. http%3A%2F%2Ftherepresentationproject.org%2Fresources%2Finfo-graphics%2Fmedia-lit%2F.

2. "Media Literacy with a Gender Lens." TheRepresentationProject.org. http://bit.ly/1BoZriq.

3. "Women's Media Center Report Finds Women Still Underrepresented, Misrepresented in U.S. Media." Women's Media Center. February 19, 2014.   www.womensmediacenter.com/press/entry/womens-media-center-report-finds-women-still-underrepresented-misrepresente.

4. Flynn, Gillian. *Gone Girl: A Novel.* New York: Crown, 2012.

5. Robinson, Tasha. "We're Losing All Our Strong Female Characters to Trinity Syndrome." The Dissolve. June 16, 2014. https://thedissolve.com/features/exposition/618-were-losing-all-our-strong-female-charac-ters-to-tr/.

6. "158 Movies Released in 2013." Listchallenges.com. http%3A%2F%2Fwww.listchallenges.com%2Fmovies-of-2013.

16. Reformed Rakes And The Radical Notion That Men And Women Are Human

1. Fein, Ellen, and Sherrie Schneider. *All the Rules: Time Tested Secrets for Capturing the Heart of Mr. Right.* New York: Warner Books, 2007.

2. Fein, Ellen, and Sherrie Schneider. *Not Your Mother's Rules: The New Secrets for Dating.* New York: Grand Central Pub., 2013.

3. Johnson, Eric M. "Promiscuity Is Pragmatic." Slate.com. December 14, 2014. http://slate.me/1CvjYHZ.

4. Cavenagh, Sarah Rose, PhD. "Female Sexual Desire: An Evolutionary Biology Perspective." *Psychology Today.* June 19, 2013. www.psychologytoday.com/blog/once-more-feeling/201306/female-sexual-desire-evolutionary-biology-perspective.

17. The Truth About Historical Accuracy

1. McRae, Elizabeth Gillespie. *Mothers of Massive Resistance: White Women and the Politics of White Supremacy.* Oxford University Press, 2018.
2. Carrie N. Baker. "Texas Republicans to Ban Public Schools Teaching History of White Supremacy: Legislators Need Their Own History Lesson." *Ms.* August 2, 2021. Accessed January 10, 2023. https://msmagazine.com/2021/08/02/texas-republicans-critical-race-theory-erin-zwiener-womens-history-white-supremacy/

18. Happy Ever After

1. Regis, 10.
2. Crusie, Jennifer. "Jennifer Crusie." Jennifer Crusie. http://www.jennycrusie.com/for-writers/essays/i-know-what-it-is-when-i-read-it-defining-the-romance-genre/.

19. Why It Matters How We Talk About Romance Novels

1. Daily, Suzanne. "Little Girls Lose Their Self-Esteem on the Way to Adolescence, Study Finds." NewYorkTimes.com. January 9, 1991. http://nyti.ms/1xv23Aq.
2. Doody, 278.

Made in the USA
Monee, IL
10 April 2023

31675353R00144